YOUR CARING HEART

RENEWAL FOR

HELPING PROFESSIONALS

AND SYSTEMS

YOUR CARING HEART

RENEWAL FOR

HELPING PROFESSIONALS

AND SYSTEMS

JAIYA JOHN

Soul Water Rising

Camarillo, California

Printed in the United States of America

Soul Water Rising
Camarillo, California
http://www.soulwater.org

Library of Congress Control Number: 2016907180
ISBN 978-0-9916401-8-8

First Soul Water Rising Edition, Softcover: 2016

Helping professionals and systems

Editors: Jacqueline V. Richmond
             Kent W. Mortensen

Cover & Interior Design: Jaiya John
Cover Photo: © Jaiya John

CONTENTS

WHO THIS BOOK IS FOR

There's this thing you do... where you care deeply enough to help people in a way that honors their humanity. I Love you for that. I just wanted to start this book by telling you. After all, you are human. The pain and suffering of others enters you. Too often, it stays. Or worse, it grows. Society does not sufficiently celebrate, compensate, or care for you. When tragedy strikes, you are frequently the first blamed. Often, you fail to receive the sensitivity and understanding you dearly need, even from family and friends. You are under enormous stress, with actual lives in your hands. You also tend to be of a deeply caring nature. So much so, that you have a tendency to neglect your own wellbeing. Here's the thing: *We need you*. You keep our human lotus blossom, our compassion, afloat. If you are going to read this book, I pray you will let your heart grow tender, and release your tears. If you do, you will have watered our sacred circle of caring.

So now... Let's define a *helping professional* as someone who provides support, directly or indirectly, to others who are in significant need. This includes volunteers. Whether you work in a hospital, prison, school, court, community clinic, or public or private agency... if you serve people in deep need, this book is for you. From the front desk, to the call center, to the IT department, to the field, if what you do affects vulnerable lives, this book is for you. If you couldn't Love your work more, or couldn't have a harder time staying with it, this book is for you. If you care deeply about this story of *Us*, or if your caring has grown weary, this book is for you.

And if you are an administrator, an executive, then you, my friend, should care about agency, worker, and leader wellness because this wellness absolutely determines the bottom line (fiscal), the top line (political), and the real line (social, generational outcomes).

As for this term, *social work*... If you are serving the social, collective human good, then regardless of title, profession, or employer, you are forever doing social work. This is meaningful because of the word *social*. The word itself points to and reminds us of our collective duty.

Welcome, you Lovers, leaders, advocates, agitators... You soul suns, deep drums, healers, hope dealers, sacred dancers. Here is a spa day for your inner peace, *birth print* for your revival, as you give yourself without celebration to the ones who dearly need your healing touch. Are you one who wades through tears, serving vulnerable lives? Please understand, you have been walking on water, staying afloat. It is okay to call yourself *Miracle Worker*.

Do you find yourself feverishly doing real, detailed work in your nighttime dreams? Is even your exhaustion exhausted? Do even your nerves have split ends? Does your workplace feel to you like a group of people furiously whacking their way through a jungle of dense paperwork vines and process overgrowth, and more than occasionally whacking at each other? Do you sometimes fantasize about slapping your coworker? Do you get the sense that your coworker may fantasize about slapping you? How about staging a revolt against management, complete with staplers as weapons? Or, if you are management, maybe putting your entire staff on timeout? Or, maybe you could not be more in Love with your work, and you wish you could infect your colleagues. If your workplace feels uninspired, combative, unsafe, overwhelming, heartbreaking, or depleting, isn't it fair to say that you, and your workplace, could use some rehabilitation and renewal? Thank you for agreeing. This writing-reading thing works better that way.

If you are a worker not in a formal leadership position, I hope you see yourself as capable of advocating for and leading change within your workplace. I have faith in this power within you. With these coming words, I speak to that power. If you are in a formal leadership position, I hope the caseworker, line staff, and administrative support staff are all alive in you. These are the informal leaders that set their groups on fire with inspiration and grace, for they carry the ember of servitude within their leadership. With these words, I address this ancient ember in you.

Please use this book to become more empowered by your own greatness. Do not become *used* by this book, growing more dependent on external guidance. I have forgotten half of what I wanted to put in these pages, so they are far from complete or absolute. And listen, as soon as this book is published, more ideas will come to me that I cringe at not having added here. Really, this book is just a mad, wandering river. But if you kneel by it and drink, something useful just might get into you. That is all.

WHAT I HAVE SEEN

I have been learning from and supporting helping professionals all of my life. The words in this book are not a prescription. They are a testimony. *Yours. Mine. Ours.* I am a witness. This is the story of what I have seen. And I have seen some things. I have seen people nearly leap across the room to strangle their coworker. I have seen professionals shaking violently with trauma, cursing uncontrollably in a venting of long denied release. I have seen lakes of tears, howls of laughter. I have seen burning bushes of anger, and the most amazing fountains of kindness. I have seen inspired leadership, and leadership lost. I have looked into so many eyes, beheld so many Loving souls, and glimpsed both profound hurt and paradises of inner peace. I have seen worker revolts, and worker revivals. And in my journey, I have never seen a workforce filled with people who do not care about their work. Something else ails us. A neglect not of the ones we serve, but a rampant untouched hurt in us that surely bleeds into our servitude. One more humbling thing I have seen: Hope. In spite of all the indecency that professionals face, all the unending chaos and drought, I have seen hope. Which is why I write these words.

CONCRETE SOLUTIONS

When I hear, "Can you please give us concrete solutions?" I hear the familiar rustling of a red flag. People also say things like: "Give us skills." You do not *give* skills, you develop them within yourself. Through practice. This *give me* culture is killing the greatness in us. *Give me* and *give us* phrases can indicate desperation, or that there may be very little or even no desire to do transformative work. Just a desire to feel better about staying the same.

Solutions? Only we can solve ourselves. The best teachers stimulate self-discovery rather than dictating rigid *solutions*. The very fluidity of life and work make *concrete solutions* an approach doomed to failure. Concrete, once poured, is hard, rigid, unmoving, and inflexible. Personal and system transformation are founded upon fluidity. Taking ideas and organically making them your own. Allowing those ideas, methods, and practices to adapt and change over time and with conditions. This is not a book of concrete solutions. It is a garden. May you get down and dirty in it and raise up some beauty.

I dream of hearing these words: "Can you please help inspire us to awaken our own greatness?" These words will tell me that someone wants to do the work. Someone cares to get down in the garden, and invest in the effort, emotion, and time necessary to bring seed to sprout, and sprout to harvest. No more "Give us..." Being *given to* does not inspire transformation. It only deepens habits of dependency and disempowerment, those old outcomes of our old system ways. What we are looking for now is a way out into a healthy reality. That way is not external to us. It exists in us, the very last place people want to go. Conventional training models have been a security blanket for us, allowing us to feel we are making honest effort to grow while avoiding the interior places where true growth becomes a sprout. One thing about despair, though, it can breed passion. In our condition, we could use some passion to finally burn down our conventional ways and surrender to work that touches the soul and renders the spirit ready for revolution. Our caring wants a system of caring that cares to be caring.

NEW DAYS

The old days are dying. For centuries, we have practiced largely autocratic, fear-based modes of serving lives. This service may have succeeded in pushing resources around. But if it were effective, we would have seen the end of generational suffering in families and communities. We haven't. We don't. We are still determined to autocratically, coldly, push resources around. This makes people in need feel pushed around. If they can't receive resources and assistance without feeling further abused, they are unlikely to find their way to healing. Nor are we, because pushing resources causes *us* to be unwell. We aren't designed to be pushers, but to be a part of something that feels good: *relationship.*

Every endemic crisis in a community is a nova reflecting a smaller firework of crisis going off inside our healers. Community crisis is not indicative of inferiority. It is the proverbial canary in the coalmine, warning us of a latent and coming crisis in systems. Systems that arise from communities like strange fruit decorating blemished trees. Social systems are in many ways the ongoing dream of generation after generation of oppressed, depressed people. Their dream carries forward that oppression and depression, which leads to laws, policies, practices, culture, mentality, and even physical environments that are oppressive and depressed.

In human and social services, depressed, autocratic leadership and *workership* is not viable. It is not working. Unless we define our objective as: *to simply push resources.* Pushers can't be healers. They're too pushy. And so, the tide has turned. The long, old era of *resourcing quantity and quota* is giving way to an era of relational quality and management of true healing. Federal and state funding incentives demand outcomes that reflect improving population health, but our systems have never been skilled at that. We have been allowed for so long to be content with service provision, not actual population health.

Public health mentality and policy have always served the socio-economic status quo. It is not a revolutionary system devoted to healing generational dysfunction and cultural oppression. But public servants and advocates can be that revolutionary force. Passionate oracles and activists have always existed among us, in these same systems, swimming upstream, resisting with every heartbeat. Who now among us knows how to achieve this new prerogative? Who wants to support the community in its healing? Let you be the ones who lead us in the work. Many of our system leaders were raised and developed in the very life and work cultures that incapacitated them from being health artisans. They may not be prepared to facilitate it in their assigned populations, not to mention in their workforce.

But health and wellness must happen in the workforce *first.* A new generation workforce has a cultural expectation and valuing of horizontal relationship, information access and sharing, transparency. This new generation of workers no longer has tolerance for abuse and neglect. They leave. Other jobs are waiting in this era of massive social need. They take with them their skills, giftedness, and spirit of wellness. One day, all that remains in your organization is people who have little spirit of wellness. People who have trouble discerning what wellness even is.

Look at us. In our systems, we take people who have a passionate calling and service gifts, and transform them into zombies consumed with looking for ways out of the work. They grow obsessed with physical and spiritual exit points. Illness manifests in their bodies, minds, and hearts. They grow calcified, crude, and cold. They are no longer servants. They are desperate pushers. And who is more destructive to a community? A single drug pusher on a street corner, or a resource pusher in a tribe of resource pushers in a resource-pushing system?

We have all seen system leaders who possess great bureaucratic intelligence and valuable, potent life and work experience. However, this does not inoculate them from lacking the emotional intelligence necessary to nurture and inspire their co-leaders and workforce into wellness. *Emotional intelligence* being the sensitivity *and desire* to tune into emotional states and operate within them.

Mountains of literature exist on leadership styles. But style is not the root issue when it comes to leadership. The root issue is personal wellness. As long as we are wracked with our own trauma, wounds, blind spots, stress, fears, and insecurities, it is difficult for any of us to blossom into a state of relational sensitivity and vision. But these are the very foundations required for a person to grow as an effective leader: Relational sensitivity. Vision. The antitheses of autocratic imposition. This matters even more because it is our leaders more than any others who show workers how to treat each other and themselves.

The old way was too rigid, controlling, and manifest in oppressive, vertical relationship. Its great cause was not to heal or be a part of healing, but to dictate, to communities and workforces. And in dictating, its arrogance was that its presumed superiority would yield a change in outcome numbers. Instead, generations of families, workers, and leaders carried forward their dysfunctions and droughts, never having been sparked into healing and transformation. They became the families, workers, and leaders of today. But this old way is dying, for the true nature in people, whether in communities or systems, is now rearing up and resisting dysfunction, like a roused immune system. And this true nature is, in the midst of despair, demanding wellness and justice, refusing to surrender hope. It is in this hopefulness that we find our way into a reality of balance, harmony, and wholeness. Shedding modes of conflict, control, and fragmentation. Demanding humanizing immersion with people and communities. Eschewing the old, cold *participation rate* compliance spirit. We know it is hope that is rising now. For only hope can produce such clamor for change.

NEW LANGUAGE

Without new language, we end up talking about the same old things in the same old ways, feeling the same as we ever did, clinging to the same old reality. The particular language in this book is not the point. What matters is the spirit and essence of healing, wellness, compassion, and servitude. If we fill our new language with the right essence, we will be on the right track. I hope the language here awakens insight in you, and that you may use it to feed your own fire for change.

WHY ORGANIZATIONS MUST CARE FOR THEIR PEOPLE

Prisons, hospitals, mental health wards, community clinics, nursing homes, schools, and social and human service agencies are the last places that should neglect caring for their workers. When an organization expects its workers to care about their work and the children and families they serve, but fails to make workers themselves feel cared for, this is a most self-defeating business practice. Wellness is contagious. So is illness. You are what you eat. As an organization, you are how you treat. Your own.

Retention has roots. Those roots precede a worker's experience with an agency, and begin with the societal story of what it means to serve those in need. Stories told in school and during professional training that introduce students to theory and practice without providing any context for visceral, generational oppression and trauma, is a story that sets up workers for failure. Failed expectations. Failed efficacy. Failed identities.

An agency caring for its workers is not an act of sacrifice. Not a favor. It is, at least, an act of self-preservation. If you care about retention and all the benefits of high retention, then caring for workers cannot escape you. Wellness is the furnace of workers' capacity to care. It is from this place and no other that they draw from their reservoir of caring. Enlightened agencies recognize that they must first and foremost protect and advocate for the wellness of their workers, and the sense of safety their climate provides. Servitude starts and ends here. We need to stop seeing conventional training as the answer to all ailments, and the way forward in change. Training is supposed to be a supplemental stream in a river of social caring, a dowry of insight in a matrimony of human technical skill and human personal relationship. Caring is the fruit or offspring of relationship. Let us no longer ask for people to care again and again in crisis and turmoil without providing them a foundation and home that feels deeply caring.

EXPOSURE

Exposure to human suffering makes your work unique. The exposure floods you from all directions: direct encounters, reading reports, phone conversations, hearing stories around the office, and from the osmosis of contact with colleagues who are themselves exposed. Because of this, the care and nurturing that happen for you and your colleagues ought to be extraordinary. Instead, it is often anemic. This has to change now, or else broken people will be serving broken people into further generations of brokenness. No. We are choosing another destiny. We shall be whole. It all starts with mutual care. It is not enough to depend on individuals to care for themselves. Our work environments themselves must be caring. This is our public duty: to offer communities *clean water* of servitude. It is not acceptable that we taint thirsty people with polluted drink. We are talking here about the purification of our servant workers, leaders, and systems. Professionals who require and deserve utmost care, for we cannot afford to lose your compassion, your language, or your light.

Your work is not insulated from what ails the world. Your work, whether in the office or field, is outside in the elements of exposure, with harsh conditions bearing down onto your naked emotional skin. This does not mean that your work is a negative thing, something to be avoided. Instead, it means that something very real and, therefore, very sacred is happening, and you are a part of it. Caring for yourself and each other, given this exposure, is not a matter of attending a training now and then, or putting self-care on your calendar. This is not marginal to your work. You would not go out in freezing weather without proper clothing. Yet we show up to our work mentally and emotionally under-fortified, perhaps numb to this exposure. Exposure that impacts us regardless. And here's another thing: Each exposure is as harmful to us as the first one was. It is a myth that the longer we do the work, the tougher and more immune we are to exposure. This is a psychological persuasion we do with ourselves that backfires. We are most Loving to ourselves when we surrender to the reality that we are vulnerable. The reality that pain and suffering do affect us, because we are caring souls. This self-talk creates an opportunity for us to act on our own behalf, and to nurture the same recognition, attitude, and *act-itude* in others.

MUTUAL CARE

The popular term *self-care* tends to evoke ideas of self-centered, individualistic, and even selfish focus. Organizations that serve vulnerable human lives are spaces far too intimate for us to care for ourselves as though we exist in an isolated vacuum. This is not a book of self-care. It is a book of mutual care. *Mutual care* is a term and concept I have been working with in recent years as I support professionals and their systems. Mutual care is not just a process. It is a cultural spirit that systems can cultivate that leads to more fruitful processes. *We are responsible for each other's wellness, regardless of position.* This is the principle at the heart of mutual care.

Mutuality... The more we peer into the depths of true wellness, the more we see relationship staring back at us. Especially when our work is relational work: being there for others in need. So let us proceed with an understanding that to care for one another is, in a very real sense, to care for ourselves. And that mutual care is ultimately a way to activate and empower our personal promise. This book is the story of our ongoing journey into mutual care. As we weave each thread of this blanket of reciprocity, we see that we are not nearly as impoverished as we may think. And that each day something hopeful rises within our collective labor that is even greater than the sun.

Mutual care is a parallel, simultaneous process. It invests in the duality present in the nature of every relationship. In doing so, it maximizes the wealth of promise existent in each relationship. It envisions staff not as powerless but powerful in their duty to support and care for themselves and their leadership. Management is held accountable for caring for itself, and for its staff. All are committed to being a relational example to the community, and to serving the community in the spirit of what is being practiced internally in the agency. However a workforce is treating itself, this is how it is liable to treat the community. Whatever we are practicing, we will administer. Service capacity is an outcome of investment in workforce wellness. Mutual care is a preparatory school for learning how to be in fruitful relationship with those we serve.

Mutual care is a fundamental foundation for wellness in an organization or group. Regardless of titles and authority positions, we are each responsible for how we care for and treat each other. It is imperative that we must develop, maintain, and protect a culture of mutual care. This value pertains to all partners in the work: communities, staff, and leadership. Each is human and need consistent, reliable care to feel safe in the circle. This is all about paying closer attention to ourselves and to each other. We can keep looking for a magic potion or wand to change our reality, or we can simply take better care.

BENEFITS OF MUTUAL CARE

Many staff will ask a fundamental question: "Why should I care to invest in a culture of mutual care?" Ultimately, for better and for worse, human beings are primarily self-serving. This is a tendency that can be used in achieving buy-in for any system change. In this case, it is important to clearly spell out the benefits (to individuals and staff as a whole) of a culture of mutual care. Here are just some of the benefits: Staff feel safer and more relaxed. Staff operate at a higher level. Staff are healthier and happier. Staff are freed to apply their giftedness. Less days lost to unwellness. Greater productivity and efficiency. Higher morale. More trust. More effective communication and understanding. Less misunderstanding and conflict. Staff and leadership feel more empowered, validated, and supported. Stronger teams and teamwork. Healthier work environment. Improved sensitivity to families and each other. Minimized impact of stress and trauma. Maximized *tribal* strengths, bonds, and wellness. Better outcomes for families. Less staff and leadership turnover. Stronger culture and continuity of values.

This is far from a comprehensive list. I encourage you to identify more benefits on your own, as you are the authority on your work's social reality. You are also a lifelong expert in the nature of reciprocity.

Mutual care is not complicated. It springs from our very nature. Think about it this way: When you were hurting the deepest, what did you need most from another human being? Was it that person's education, training, or paperwork? Or, was it that person's compassion? Most likely, your deepest need was that someone care. Deeply. If this is what you needed when you were hurting, be that for every soul. For each coworker and service recipient. Each day, in every moment, we can choose to be medicine or malice for the world. Be medicine, and you will inherit a life and vocation that is medicinal for you in return.

AUTHENTICALLY HONOR CULTURE

Mutual care is a value that honors cultural integrity. Culture, as in *a person's way of being*. Beyond ancestral, a people's way of being extends to the granularities of how they learn, heal, teach, use technology, pay attention, participate in discussions and meetings, communicate, problem solve, and create. This granular expanse within an organization, and within communities, is as rich in stories as is a beach with grains of sands. Mutual care takes care not only of people, but also of their cultural integrity. It holds them together in their natural wholeness and context, and in doing so, mutual care holds the *tribe* together. Not in a gentrified homogeneity of dominant culture, but in a sacred intimacy of being fully human. *Me comprendes?*

WHAT IS THE HEALING WORK TO BE DONE?

It is amazing how often agencies go all the way through funding and rolling out a change initiative without ever first clarifying the root issue. For various reasons, we tend to avoid this step like the plague. Fear, confusion, insecurity, and misunderstanding are among the reasons for this omission. Usually a system is filled with tremendous levels of grievance and frustration, but very little insight into the actual process of change.

It helps to first identify the pathology. What is it that ails us? Imagine if a team of doctors took over the case of a patient with cancer and never paused to identify the type of cancer. The entire treatment mentality and approach would not only be uninformed, it would be reckless and likely harmful. And yet, we see systems repeatedly proceeding in this manner.

So, what is our pathology? Systems need to find the courage, reason, and will to ask this question to the entire workforce and community in an empowering manner, space, and process. What do we know doesn't work? Colonial imposition of executive leadership's idea of the pathology onto a process the workforce and community had little role in shaping.

Forums, surveys, and other feedback loops can be useful, but too often these means are polluted with gatekeepers' presumptions of what the issue is and how to address it. In other words, even in asking the question to workers and community, we tend not to grant them the sincerity of honoring their input. Commonly, systems already have their initiative in place, and only then, as a matter of show or token consideration, ask the key partners for their opinion and insight. In a romantic relationship, this kind of approach would be considered condescending, controlling, manipulative, self-serving, and even narcissistic.

What then are healthful, productive ways to assess the pathologies, dysfunctions, and needs to be addressed? Through honest relationships. Whether one-on-one or collective, honest relationships yield honest input. Now, if your environment does not have many honest relationships, which is itself a reflection of pathology, then the work may need to start with the healing of personal work relationships. As these relationships mend and emerge, they become the assessment method and input vessel to feed the vision of how the agency is to become well.

Only through organic spaces and connections do people begin to feel that they are being heard and honored in an authentic manner that has a hope of leading to change. If all of the assessment methods are cold, clinical, and formal, this douses the sense of intimacy and genuine care that encourages honest feedback. Spontaneous, warm sharing in personable, *tribal time* moments helps beaten-down people feel the first stirrings of empowerment.

Once systems have created sincere invitation and permission to share input into pathology and need, they need to learn how to effectively gather the collective story. And then learn how to interpret meaning from this story. Here is where skilled individuals, whether internal or external to the system, can be of help. Some people's superpower is to take a multitude of voices and recognize patterns within the mass. Systems can use people like this.

Ultimately, patience and attentiveness are what bring a system to accurate identification of root pathologies and need. Paradoxically, patience and attentiveness can be in short supply in a traumatized, stressed, rushed culture and climate. So this assessment stage requires a critical number of people who are willing to push back against the impatience, anxiety, and panic. People who can say, "Let's dig deep and get this right."

BEING HUMAN

Historically, leaders in our fields have been discouraged from teaching and encouraging so-called *soft skills*. This is ironic because these are the skills of compassionate relationship that are rhetorically the very capstone value of systems that serve vulnerable people. We are suffering from the consequence of this contradiction. To communities and workers, the contradiction feels like hypocrisy. It is time to stop idolizing *hard skills* (cold, technical service provision) as the centerpiece of what we do. And it is time to rename *soft skills* as, *being human*. When people ask us what we do as professionals and systems, we should be able to honestly say, "We are all about being human with each other." Healing is an acutely personal and private affair. When we need it, the support we receive should be intimate, even if the resources offered are clinical or material. We work in intimacy. This is our trade and craft, our skillset and spirit.

PRACTICE IS THE BEST *BEST PRACTICE*

This is a book that celebrates the art of practice. I have seen a great reluctance in us to practice the things necessary for change to happen. We want someone to ride in on a magic horse, wave a magic wand, speak magic words, and magically make our whole work reality better. This is magical thinking. It doesn't do much for change. Even when we are exposed to promising ideas, we are reluctant to truly practice them. Then we come back and think: *That idea was great in theory, but in my absolutely, tremendously, incredibly horrible reality, that idea is not realistic. I have real work to do.* Funny, we are.

We won't practice. Not effectively enough. Not often enough. Not long enough. We just want to be able to say that the idea didn't work. That way we can settle back into our way of being, and complain our day away. Did you ever notice that some people resent it when their reason to complain is taken away? Bless their hearts. Grow comfortable enough inside a complaining spirit and you too will resent someone pulling you into a spirit of contentment. That's a tug of war that can go on for years.

Speaking of which, our *practice calendar* expectations can be unrealistic. We expect a problem worker or system culture to be cured in weeks or maybe months, or even after one heart-to-heart conversation. This is not how change works. Dysfunctional ways are embedded in us like a root system. Our actions and attitudes are like the trees emerging from those roots. The roots include hurt, trauma, unattended need, and misguided understanding. Transforming these roots takes time. These may not be lifelong projects, but they at least involve consistent attention over numerous months. We need to strengthen the muscles of our new habits, for those muscles keep us in the habit. We create habits through repetition. Rituals, ceremonies, and traditions, hallmarks of true tribes, solidify our practices until they become instinctive and cultural. They also shape our personal and group identities.

An idea, book, symposium, conference, or seminar can be genius in its inspiration. But this doesn't matter if people or groups aren't willing to invest in practice. Not practice for a little while, or until the funding cycle runs out. Practice as an integrated part of the work. Permanently. Practice is the act and art of doing something repeatedly. *Resistance x Repetition = Change*. The resistance is the force of doing something new, which creates a rebellion by the preexisting habit, whether mental or behavioral. Thus, resistance. It is the old habit that is resisting. It will continue to do so, perhaps forever, since its seed will remain in us, waiting for us to stop practicing.

There is no magical piece of paper, hammer, wand, or other external "tool" that will create personal or collective change. We cannot be empowered without our own sincere effort to grow. Changing our work reality depends upon our internal transformation, so that *we* become the most reliable, enduring, effective tool in our self-leadership. This requires that we commit to daily practice of the attitudes and behaviors we desire, so that they can become deep habits. And remember... *Best Practice* assumes that we are practicing.

YOUR TRIBE

I hesitate to use the word *tribe*. It has been culturally appropriated, shorn of origin and meaning. Made into fashion. Still, I choose to use the word *tribe*. As an aspirational vision that I believe carries our necessary direction forward. I use the word because in the most Indigenous of ways, a tribe is an ancestral people, with ancestral memory, existing in wholeness and harmony with the world, in a spirit of being true humans. Our modern, professional gatherings of born servant souls, helpers, and healers, are very much ancestral. We absolutely carry ancestral memory of what it means to be in harmony and wholeness. To walk what the Diné call *Nizhoní, The Beauty Way*. And so, I will use the word *tribe*.

Something more than employment must be in place to hold a group or organization together. Specifically, strong, cohesive groups invest in *nurtured relationships* and *common cause*. These qualities are present in the historical cultural concept that we can call a *tribe*. A tribe does not exist as a means of materialism. It exists by virtue of relationship tinctured in a spirit of working toward a common cause. Indigenously, this cause is the wellness of all beings in the circle of life. Harmony is valued greatly, both within the tribe and in relation to the natural world the tribe itself exists to serve.

Organizations and systems that serve human lives ought to, ideally, exist and operate as tribes: with a deep conviction for relationship and harmony as a means to deliver the care, services, and resources that people need. Note that I initially indicated *nurtured relationships*. Obviously people who work together are in relationship. This does not assure that the relationships are healthy or in harmony. Without a programmatic and mission commitment to nurturing relationships, we might as well be saying to trauma and dysfunction, "*Come right on in. You're welcome here.*" And without a common cause, even nurtured relationships can struggle, lose steam, and wander, lacking true purpose and direction.

In work where we have been conditioned to believe that we are only supposed to serve the community, and not ourselves, we need organizational encouragement to lean on each other as peers for support. Whether this comes through training, change initiatives, or mentoring, it is necessary that a climate emerge that emphasizes peer support as central to our work.

How do we know that our organization values nurtured relationships and common cause? Because we can find both dynamics operating freely and continuously beyond the programming calendar. If staff and leadership can only find an issue on a calendar or as an agenda item, this sends a clear message right away: *This item is not a part of the real work for which I am here. It is marginal, an additive. It is not of me or for me, so I have no need to own it.* The psychology of ownership says that if you do not make a thing central to people's existence, they will not be motivated to own it as a part of their existence.

Continuity, consistency, and centrality: these are the traits by which a group proves its priority. A tribe is a tribe not because the word *tribe* is cool, or because tribal culture has been fetishized. A tribe is a tribe because it proves its relational and *common cause* priority over and again, generationally, through its daily life and work. Its spirit of value is so potent and ritualized that you can fathom its ancestral, generational quality. You can feel, see, smell, hear, taste, and touch a strong tribe's relational, purposeful essence. Your workplace can be like this.

TRIBAL MYTHS

Our human service work is saturated in countless tribal myths: You must be grim, stressed, and serious when serving lives. Organizations must be dank, dour, and depressing environments. No sunlight allowed. No music or soothing colors. Wellness, kindness, and compassion are trivial focuses. Processes and procedures are the real work. Self-care is a fantasy. Laughing, crying, and all forms of being human are prohibited. New workers must be brought into line by the tenured workers. Tenured workers must be not be inspired by new workers. Leaders must bully in order to lead. The longer we have been doing something that makes no sense, the more necessary it is that we continue not making sense. Only something outside of ourselves can save us. In the face of crisis, we must ourselves be in crisis, or else we are insensitive. The list goes on...

To destroy a harmful myth, we need to start a helpful myth. A myth can be truthful or untruthful. In the end, it doesn't matter. What matters is that the myth exists. To eradicate it, something needs to fill the space left behind, or the old myth will return to fill in the space. It's like digging out a sandcastle moat at the beach. Sea water keeps seeping back into the space you just dug out, until you fill that space with something solid. What tribal legend can you and your team create that is solid? That holds meaning, truth, and wellness? If we do not ask the question, we will never arrive at the beautiful legend. Bless each other with daily meals of real stories. Ones that start with, "This really happened to me..." Real stories help counteract tribal myths and personal misunderstandings about the work. Real stories are reassuring even if they involve jeopardy or challenge. It is the realness that makes people feel: *If they can go through that, I can, too.*

MARTYRS

Private, and especially public organizations, are greatly shaped by public pressure. Their persona comes to reflect the chronic weight bearing of outside influences: Boards of supervisors. Media. Community leaders, boards, and initiatives. As a result, agencies believe their public accountability means that providing any comforts to workers is a sin. But workers are serving comfort, not paperwork, to families and children in crisis. How can workers continue serving comfort if they are not allowed to be comfortable?

Those who serve lives, their leaders, and their culture have in many ways informally agreed to take on the role of martyrdom. We say, "If our children and families are suffering, we must suffer, too. Everyone will go without water, food, sunlight, kindness, health, or intimacy from this day forward. We will show that we take suffering seriously." Examining this martyrdom consciousness, we see that it renders us all unconscious. We no longer think with a mind of wellness. In its place we exercise a mind of suffering. This is not what hurting communities need from us. They need us to be practitioners of peace, stability, and prosperity.

The public does not wish for us to suffer with them. They wish for us to be with them in their suffering. Big difference. Moreover, they need us to be with them in a healing manner. Not a resource-pushing manner. A healing manner.

MASTERS

We are trained by our entire life and all its relationships that to be a leader is to be a master. Many of us never examine this myth. Suddenly we are responsible for dozens, hundreds, thousands of workers, and all the souls they serve. Situated in this pressure cooker, we turn up the valve of doing whatever masters do. We go about mastering. Unfortunately, with each pulse of this practice, we are further lost from mastering peace: Peace within. Peace all around. This is what true leaders cultivate. For only in a state of peace can a person, team, or tribe be said to be in a state of ultimate servitude. Only in peace can our giftedness fully flow and flower.

But we go about mastering, which we believe means we need to control something. Anything. Anxiously, we grasp for things to control: people, processes, language, climate. Given that control of the world is one of the most destructive myths, our control impulses only succeed in causing us to lose control as a leader. How do we resolve this problem? By learning how not to be a master. All around us are people, at work and in our lives, who have mastered *not mastering*. They practice relationship. Harmony. Mutuality. Peace. None of them is charging a fee for their class. Sign up. Humble the master. Be a student. Even the biggest bully can learn to be a student.

One step on the path of true, compassionate leadership is forgiveness. Forgive your learning curve. Forgive your fears and insecurities. Speak to them out loud, Lovingly. Reassure them. Place them on the fire of your personal transformation. Hold a ceremony. Let them burn.

THE NATURE OF BEING A SOCIAL SERVANT

Several years ago, I was part of a gathering in the far eastern New Mexico desert involving social service professionals from the Diné (Navajo) Nation. It was a strong circle, with stories shared and warmth passed around. Good medicine was flowing. At some point in the proceedings, an elder came to the front of the room. He said, "I would like to share with you here in this circle the history of social service in the Diné tradition."

He said to us, "When a child is born, we say, 'She has been born for our people. For her clan. Not *from* or *of*, but *for*. This *for* implies purpose, which in turn implies value. When a child grows up hearing from her people that she was born for something, this constant rain of purpose deepens her sense of self-worth, esteem, identity, and reason for being well. She knows her people need her. That she must find and celebrate her gifts, and fulfill her calling. This is the root of a resilient, high coping human being."

The Diné elder continued: "At first, we her people, pay close attention to her behavior and attitudes, for they are signs to us of her calling. Before she has even learned to walk, we watch for her signs. She may be crawling around with other infants. When one of them starts to cry, we watch for her response. Does she crawl toward tears and suffering, or does she crawl away?

"As she grows, we continue watching for her purpose. One day, she may be playing with other children when a fight breaks out. We watch. Does she wade into conflict and make war? Or does she wade into conflict and make peace?

"Later, still a child, we may find her in a school or community setting when an injustice occurs. We are watching. Does she stand up against the injustice and for justice, or does she hold back and let injustice have its way?

"We the people have been raised in our culture to understand our responsibility: to behold the child, the new life, and witness what this spirit tells us about her purpose and calling. When we see that the child crawls toward tears and suffering, wades into conflict and makes peace, and stands up against injustice and for justice, we know a social servant, a healer has been born for us.

"But this is not the end of our duty. Once we realize who she is, we now know we must address a fundamental vulnerability of social servants. Because they were born to care so deeply for others, to be so consumed in setting the world right, mending the ruptures, social servants are also more likely to neglect themselves. Our duty as a people (team, unit, organization, community) is to nurture in her a priority and habit for self-care. For tending to her own garden, so that many may continue to feed themselves from her provision of caring. This is the true meaning of social service for our Diné people: a collective responsibility to care for one another, to support our respective vulnerabilities."

These words from the elder that day in the desert have stayed with my spirit, shaping my way of seeing our personal and collective wellness work. We each have certain qualities that make us gifted for the work. These same qualities can also leave us vulnerable to *unwellness*, if we do not take care.

Years ago, I spent a great deal of time doing work supporting youth, families, and professionals in the New Orleans area. This was before Hurricane Katrina. I was blessed with wonderful relationships with so many vibrantly spirited people. Especially the social service professionals. The helpers. One year after the hurricane and flood, I was asked to return to be part of their one-year anniversary commemoration of the tragedy, the loss, and the healing. On a hot, humid late August day, I stood at the pulpit in an historic African American church, reciting a healing poem in tribute to the New Orleans community. Many tears flowed, filling the pews and air with abundant soul.

As our gathering moment in the church passed, several folks shared with me stories of the preceding year. A central story emerged. One of courage and sacrifice. You may have heard of the thousands of people stranded in the Superdome during the flood. The Superdome is a large football stadium, home to the NFL's New Orleans Saints. For too many days following the initial hurricane, in the midst of terrible flooding, droves of people were stranded inside the Superdome, waiting in terror. The climate in the Dome was oppressive. Late summer heat and humidity were stifling. Children crying in despair. Dead bodies lying around under sheets. Sick and wounded people. The smells and suffocating, claustrophobic atmosphere. The not knowing. *The not knowing.*

A year later, in the church, I heard a collage of stories about the numerous social servants who had stayed behind to help those stranded in the Dome. In many cases, these workers had the opportunity to evacuate the area, to relocate around the country as so many others had. Their employers granted them permission and work leave. Yet, one after another, they had chosen the response in harmony with their true nature. They had stayed. And now, a year later, I was hearing about how so many of them, the helping professionals, had tragically died over the following months. Died of heart attacks, strokes, and other maladies resulting from the acute stress of the Dome and the chronic stress of their lives thereafter. Lives in which they had gone back to work, continuing to serve, without ever taking or receiving the opportunity to tend to their horrific grief, loss, and trauma. They had died young. In the energetic primes of their 30's to 60's. They had died at a greater rate than those they had stayed in the Dome to serve. This truth is evidence of the vulnerability of which the Diné elder spoke in the desert.

I have seen this truth play out in my own life and in so many lives of helping professionals around the country and world. Over the last several years, this truth, this vulnerability and unwellness outcome, has emerged as the almost exclusive need for which my services have been requested by agencies and organizations. Workers, supervisors, managers, and executive leadership are all seeing and often grudgingly submitting to this same panorama.

We have hit a collective wall. People and systems are breaking down. We can go no further with our neglect of being whole in servitude. Our mainstream culture is unhealthy. Our service cultures are unhealthy. We who serve are unhealthy. And yet, the natural laws of wellness have never left us. The path home remains the same. And in this truth, there is much promise.

THE GREEN MILE

The first time I watched the movie, *The Green Mile*, starring Tom Hanks and Michael Clarke Duncan, tears flooded my face. I saw myself in the central character, John Coffey. And no, not just because he was a massive, bald, Black man. John Coffey had a gift. He was a healer. He could touch people and take their pathology from them and into himself. From cancer, to bladder infection, to death and even scalding hatred, John Coffey relieved all of it. But this wasn't why I saw myself in his character. It was because after each of John Coffey's acts of compassion and healing, the mountainous man was left beyond exhausted. His giant body would collapse onto his prison cell cot. As he collapsed, he would call out to Tom Hanks' prison guard character, weakly intoning, "So tired, Boss. So tired."

The only way that John Coffey could be well again was to release the pathology he had taken into himself from the previously ailing person. The movie showed this process graphically. His entire torso, shoulders, and face lifted toward the sky, he coughed and heaved. Then he regurgitated what looked like a swarm of bees or moths that gushed upward in a buzzing vortex, dispersing in the air. Only after this release was John Coffey able to restore himself. It seems as though many helping professionals and healer souls are John Coffey. Forever taking in the toxicity and torment of others. Driven by Love and compassion. By a calling. The jeopardy is that too often such people do not release what they have taken in. John Coffey's exhaustion is labeled in our contemporary culture as vicarious trauma, burnout, and compassion fatigue.

Being affected in such a way can cause a person to develop a negative association with being open, with taking in the suffering of others. We may tell ourselves: *This is too much. Caring like this is killing me.* But is caring the culprit? Is the essential nature of the work the problem? Humans have always suffered. Healers have always been called to the suffering. Perhaps what we have lost over time is the cultural knowledge and practice of *releasing.* Maybe our work and our bureaucracy is not the key cause of our ailing and exhaustion. If we have lost our tether to what it means to renew and replenish, or if we never had the tether to begin with, we are missing half of our servitude gift.

OUR CAPACITY TO RECEIVE SUFFERING AND GIVE LOVE

Our capacity to receive is directly related to the work we do to create inner space for receiving. Sleep deprivation, emotional disturbance, worry, stress, anger, distraction, rushing against time... all of these factors and more impede our ability to receive the lives of others. And this is what our work is, is it not? To receive the lives of coworkers, care recipients, family, friends, and strangers. And our capacity does not distinguish between types of people. If we are feeling overwhelmed or topped off, this affects the way we receive anyone and everyone.

If we do not clear out space in our home, we cannot keep adding belongings. If we do not clear out space in our emotional, energetic body, we become cluttered and cannot take on any more. This is when we react by closing down, becoming less caring and kind, and treating others more harshly. Patience is not a static quantity. It is a fluid capacity directly resulting from our inner housekeeping.

Giving Love and compassion is not a fixed trait, determined by our nature. It is an impulse influenced by our state of being. It is not that we have less to give, but that we are increasingly blocked in our giving nature. Remember, an open faucet flows naturally. So does an open *you.*

COMPASSION FATIGUE

"Do not think that love in order to be genuine has to be extraordinary. What we need is to love without getting tired. Be faithful in small things because it is in them that your strength lies."

Mother Teresa

Compassion fatigue is a misnomer. A misunderstanding. It is not possible for compassion, or Love, to become fatigued. What fatigues is the human being who loses compassion. Mother Teresa, bless her soul, might have been a Jedi. Maybe she used mind tricks on herself. How else to explain her ability not to become overwhelmed by the sheer mass of human suffering she and her Sisters of Charity waded into and remained faithfully beside? Actually, she herself offered a simpler explanation. She believed that as long as she drew, in her work, from her infinite well of Love and compassion, she would have infinite energy and endurance to serve. She believed that it is when we fall into the trap of operating from the mind, from the ego field of information and intellect that we swiftly grow exhausted.

Sister Teresa was often asked how she sustained herself being immersed in so many millions of suffering, impoverished lives, for so many years. She was known to answer in ancient Greek, pointing to one person at a time and saying, "Ek. Ek. Ek." *From out of that one. That one. That one.* She believed that if she touched one drop of the ocean, she was touching the entire ocean, and that the entire ocean was touching and restoring her. This is a great practice tool. We become overwhelmed with seemingly endless caseloads, perceiving too little time and too few resources with which to resolve our cases. When feeling overwhelmed, we can calm and empower ourselves with Mother Teresa's mantra. *This one person. All I have to do is give what I have in this moment to this one. This is all I can do. This is enough.* There is a tried and true psychology to breaking the whole down into manageable parts. Not divisible parts. Interdependent parts. Touch the drop, touch the ocean.

Mother Teresa made it clear throughout her life that the only reason she could sustain her energy and wellness, and the only reason she was able to make any difference at all, was not because of her intelligence, education, or practice skills. It was because of her Love. Without Love, we are not serving, we are imposing. Our efforts land harshly, leave bruises, and diminish the potential that exists in every human connection.

BURNOUT

When we say we are burned out on the work, is this true? How do we know it is the work itself that caused the burnout? Is it possible that *our relationship to the work* may be a cause? And how are we defining the work we say has burned us out? Does our definition include things not intrinsic to the work? If so, does this mean it may be possible to amend our statement, to begin saying that particular things have burned us out? If so, if we can grow more accurate in recognizing our burnout factors, we have hope of better treating the burnout.

With burnout, it is helpful to encourage staff not to only take time off, but also time out, and time in. Time out involves stepping away from or outside of the present task or environment, to calm, compose, and center ourselves. Time in is that act of being present with ourselves, becoming our own best company. It is meditative, reflective, and self-connective. Time *off, out,* and *in* can all be useful, especially as we learn to use them together.

Some things can be removed from the work. Some things cannot. Of those that can be removed, have we, personally and together, done all that we can to eradicate those elements? Maybe we think we have, but upon closer, honest inspection, we see we can do more. Of the things that cannot be removed, can we change our relationship to those things? Almost always. This answer threatens our ego, but this fact does not change the answer. *Almost always.* Our relationship to all things is at least partially shaped by our perceptions and attitudes, which are ever amendable. We can pitch a fit and say, "I'm not trying any longer. They aren't trying," and then see how that approach helps. We can also grow hard-headed and say, "I will never stop working on what I can control, which is my way of seeing and being." This stubborn determination can be its own beautiful revolution.

DISILLUSIONMENT AND DESPAIR

When we lose hope, the tonic is new hope. All ailments reveal their cure in their very nature. Disillusionment and despair are not just unfortunate states. They are also indicators. They suggest what is missing. When we learn to appreciate the face of unwellness as a window into wellness, we grow more comfortable with and secure in the full range of human expression. We become cultivators, working with whatever presents itself to us, whether it comes from us or others.

When we grow despairing it is only because we have a wonderful need not to despair. This makes despairing an opportunity: It can show us that what is particularly needed are the conditions that cause despairing to go away. What are those conditions? We need only think about our own moments of despair, or those of people in our life. What helped? That answer is likely at least part of our present-moment answer. Despair is not an endpoint. It is the beginning of understanding how to create conditions in which our tribe does not despair. Hope, faith, trust, honesty, kindness, purpose, meaning, consistency... all are just some of the countless seeds for a system garden where despair does not grow.

ENTERING THE TRIBE

Three points of vulnerability and opportunity exist in your work life. When you enter the tribe (organization), while you exist in the tribe, and as you leave the tribe. As you enter the tribe, you bring with you both beauty and baggage. Offerings and pollution. No judgment here, just the human truth. Fruitful organizations pay attention to your season of entry. They don't push you through a careless hiring and orientation process. They initiate you into the culture. Not everybody belongs in a Loving culture, though everyone could use one.

Are you one of those who showed up, fresh out of college or graduate school, or another industry, eager and excited to help people? Were you flush with idealism and energy, brimming with the audacious belief that you could change the world? If this was you, or is you at the moment, just starting your career, you are one of many.

Hopefully your story does not go like this: new worker, spilling over with smiles and positivity, shows up for the first day of work. She can't wait to learn this work from the amazing people she knows must be part of her new tribe. She bounces into the office and is greeted by... a tribe full of tired, burned out, hurting, disillusioned trolls and goblins. Each of them possesses a most wondrous heart, a heart that has been buried under sediment of stress and trauma. These weary workers react with something like horror to the smiles and positivity of the new worker. They caution her: "Girrrrl... You better get your act together. You need to become more jaded, or you're never going to make it around here. This ain't no place for smiles and optimism. Check that mess at the door."

The new worker is stunned. Deflated. She thought she was joining a tribe of joyful helpers. Instead, she has been greeted by and initiated by a culture of grim reapers. Within weeks and months, she has begun to lose her shine. She feels lost, asking herself: *Is this the place for me?* Discouraged from being kind and caring, she does her best to fit in. She suppresses her natural openness and warmth. Adopts a hard outward composure. Her facial features, once soft, grow harsh. Her body language stiffens and closes, along with her heart. This allows stress to balloon inside of her. The pressure damages her body, her brain, her whole being. She no longer wakes excited to go to work. Dread sets in. She does her best to settle into the dread, to make her way day by day. On the day of her one-year anniversary, her unit throws her a party. She eats a cupcake in a state of surreal dislocation from herself. Colleagues congratulate her on fitting in so well to her new tribe.

Your own initiation in to this work and its workplaces should feel Loving, welcoming, and honoring. You should be showered with nutritional tribal stories, just as you would be showered with leis in Hawaiian culture. We're striving for an *Aloha* kind of welcome here. Your work demands it. If your entry experience is what it should be, you are well prepared in attitude, emotion, and most of all, relationship. Your initial relationships are vital in inoculating and insulating you from harmful work elements, igniting your natural gifts, and opening you for the relational nature of your work. If this description doesn't match your entry story, see what you can do to ensure a more positive entry story for someone else joining the tribe right now, or who will very soon. We assume new staff can magically figure out our group culture on their own. They can't. Not all of it. Be helpful. Introduce them to the unspoken things. Help them learn the common song. This will help them feel that they belong.

BEING IN THE TRIBE

Life in your workplace tribe brings with it elements that build you and those that wear on you. Hopefully, more of the former than the latter. If you feel that aspects of the culture are harmful, never tell yourself that you can't do anything about it. This inner voice invites helplessness, a state that leaves you more vulnerable to stress, crisis, and trauma. Instead, work to stay in activist mode. Your workplace culture is not a static, unchanging thing, or a single-cell organism. There is no single power-that-be. Your tribal culture is a fluid, transitive creature, ebbing and flowing with each person, and with the changes within each person. Remind yourself of this. You will feel more able and hopeful about your role and influence. Keep your colleagues in conversation about the culture. What do you all notice changing? What is the meaning of these changes? What has been lost? What can be found? Keep this awareness story aloft, the way a circle of people might keep a beach ball or balloon in the air. When the story comes bouncing to you, send it back out with all the influence you choose to put into it. Your greatest duty at work is not to survive, but to affect the climate. To leave a healthy imprint, in your own image. In fruitful groups, each person takes responsibility for the air that all are breathing. Communities evolve. Systems honor communities by evolving with them. The vital seed in this ceremony of change is you.

LEAVING THE TRIBE

If, for whatever reason, you find yourself leaving your organization, show the same care for those relationships that you did prior. Show care by sharing your stories and lessons. Do this strategically.

See if your insights and feedback can be gathered and used by the group as it goes forward. Pay attention to other people leaving. What are they taking with them in terms of value, skills, and gifts? See that your group talks about this. Discuss how you might replace what has been lost, and not just through the hiring process. Reexamine roles and relationships. Allocate time and attention for nurturing the tenderness and absence left behind when people leave. Leaving is not necessarily a negative for your group or agency. Leaving is a form of change, which means that opportunities also emerge. When children go off to college, parents do themselves a favor by honestly appraising their new season of life. Intentional changes are made. This appraisal can also happen in your workplace, formally and informally. Each day, it is worth asking together: *Who are we today?* Reality changes daily. So should the subtleties of our identity.

TRIBAL TIME

A particular drought we suffer is not spending enough intimate time together in person. To the point that some of us have grown uncomfortable with such intimacy. But togetherness can be like slipping into hot bath water: uncomfortable at first, but soon enough our bones begin to purr. To cure this drought of togetherness, let's create reasons to be together, until it becomes a habit again.

We also need genuine, informal, intimate time together, whether face-to-face or in communication. Let's call this *tribal time*. Tribal time is when we get to connect with each other heart and soul, in laughter or tears, and just be real. It is a space that allows for and encourages us to share, receive, learn, be affirmed, commiserate, and support each other. Elder and tenured members share their wisdom. Young and new workers share their energy and enthusiasm. We draw social support. We grieve together, remember together, learn together. During tribal time we release, let go, discover, clarify, solidify, and honor. Space is provided for ritual, ceremony, and tradition, all of which crystallizes and solidifies new habits. Tribal time honors our work by nurturing the soul of those who do the work. This may seem foreign to old, weary cultural work systems, but it is familiar wherever humans gather in vibrant, productive communion. Tribal time is as important to a workforce as family time is to a family. It is an intimacy that holds us together, heals us, and carries us forward.

People grow fatigued of *trainings*. Maybe because training is so often linear: You come, sit, receive information. Maybe we are burned out on information. Inspiration might be what we need. And not just *interactive exercises*. We need heart-to-heart sharing. Regularly. In informal spaces and moments. We need to be free for seconds and minutes here and there, just to connect with each other humanly. Tribal time is vastly different from the often inert, uninspired time spent together during typical training sessions. Tribal time is riotous in its eagerness to do creative work together. In tribal time, work groups are not obsessed with system tasks, but with creative kinship and bonding. Spend time together outside of work, or at least outside of your designated workgroup. Doing so refreshes the spirit, gives the mind a break, and lets *social letting go* do what it does to stress and isolation. Get outside yourself in ways that make going back within yourself feel like a warm welcome home.

Within work tribes, cohorts have great power, which they usually keep to themselves. Seasoned cohorts have a duty to share with new cohorts what they witnessed and learned. New cohorts have a duty to advocate to seasoned cohorts for guidance and initiation. Your seasons have reasons. Make use of them.

If you are a formal leader, go out into the field with your staff. If you are staff, invite your leaders to ride along. This builds relationship and trust, and sensitizes leaders to the service realities of their staff.

Simple physical features around the office can be cultivated into tribal gathering spots. The water cooler, the coffee pot, an open area by a large window, a spot by a tree outside, any common areas. During our K-12 schooling we were taught that social gathering was mostly bad, that there was serious school work to do and that gathering only led to trouble. Now that we are adults, we need to unlearn this idea. Instead of discouraging staff from gathering, we should encourage it. Gathering is primal. It is a sign of people needing something to satisfy their social nature, to release tension or find communion and comfort. So, let us gather.

TRIBAL CHECK-IN

The way we greet each other matters. It is an initiation into the moment, a statement of care. Saying "Good Morning" goes a long way toward making someone's morning good. Funny, right? Before your team members leave the office for the evening, and when they arrive in the morning, care to check in with them. See how they are doing. Greet and embrace them. You never know what personal life someone is coming from or returning to. Wish them well over the weekend, or prior to vacation. Welcome them back warmly after the weekend, on a regular morning, or after they have been out sick. You have word power. Use it. We all need abundant social support, regardless of position. When staff figure out that by nurturing their formal leaders, the nurturing returns to them exponentially, things can really change. Another thing: Support means different things to different people. It helps to ask people how you can best support them.

This doesn't have to be the Spanish Inquisition. Just naturally care to see how people are doing. Sense how much they need to share, then honor their need. Allow yourself the same. Let yourself be checked-into. It's not just for you. It's also for the peace of the tribe. Healthy tribes check in with each other, spontaneously and ritually. If you happen to run into someone in the building, or while moving through a staff meeting, that moment is a tool. Use it to check in with them. They will feel more at home and safe. Your bond will be stronger, and you will be more sensitive and aware.

THE STORY WE TELL OURSELVES

How well do you know your own heart? Your own soul? Is your idea of *you* empowering you or disempowering you? Is this idea illuminating your true self, or is it highlighting a false idea of you? A false idea constructed during childhood by family, friends, society, and fears? Your story is not a linear, chronological narrative. It has no start or end. It is a circle. A patchwork quilt composed of every thought, idea, belief, and feeling you have chosen to keep or failed to examine.

If we tell a story enough times, it ceases to be just a story. Now, it is our reality. Psychology literature has been clear for decades: When it comes to human beings, what we *perceive* to be real is in effect our reality. Therefore, the story we tell ourselves is the soundtrack that determines our experience. This is true for our story about work, about those we serve, about those we lead or are led by, and about ourselves as persons. Our story is so powerful that it overrides actual reality and becomes the driving force behind our feelings, attitude, outlook, and hopefulness or hopelessness.

Once we accept that everything is a story, we begin to become mindful storytellers. Who in your group or organization is gathering the stories? Who is preserving them? Who is examining them? Who is telling them? Are these people acting in the direction of collective healing and wellness, or in the direction of dysfunction? We are best served by choosing each of our story role takers wisely. In a small group, you and your colleagues can ask yourselves: "What is our story of how we treat each other? Does this story match our reality?" Talk about what your reality needs to be, then make sure your story begins to be in harmony with that standard.

The stories we tell ourselves about who we are, who we are in the work, who we are as a peer team, and as an agency, are the root of creating either a healthful, positive climate, or a traumatized, dysfunctional one. Everything from recruitment, hiring, retention, professional development, and programming should involve the nurturing, practicing, and protecting of our positive, healthy stories.

NURTURE YOUR STORY

We nurture our personal and collective stories by sharing them. Not periodically. Regularly. Talk as a unit or team about what went well today, this week, this month, or this year. Share your positive personal stories with each other. We have no idea who among our group will be touched or inspired by what's going on in our personal life. As a team, celebrate your casework success stories with other teams. Units starve each other of joyful, triumphant stories when they should be feeding each other. This is the unfortunate fact of territorial mindsets and cultures. Burn that culture to the ground. A story carries light and hope, just what professionals need in this work. Pass the torch. Create a tradition within each concentric social circle at your workplace: Have people volunteer to be the storyteller for the month. Let them go around collecting stories. In the process, they fertilize relationships between workgroups.

Find creative ways to transmit your stories. New technology ways. Old school ways. Circulate a newsletter that collects and shares exclusively positive, celebratory stories. When people see this newsletter in their inbox, they will gravitate toward it like a dune beetle to water in the desert. I just made that up. I don't even know anything about dune beetles. I assume they get thirsty.

Regularly produced newsletters and ongoing social media streams help irrigate and fertilize relationships, lessons, wisdom, and morale. Newsletters work even better when we keep them full of zest and spirit. Monotonous reporting is not the point. Entertain as you share information. Throw a party inside your new edition.

Our human brain likes to be provided a clear picture of things. Here is a helpful question to ask the people you serve, and each other: "When it goes well, what does it look like?" The *It* could be a case, a crisis resolution, a conversation, a promotion. It might be a reunion or meeting, a presentation, or social gathering. All sorts of *Its* are happening every day. Examine them to determine what went well, and paint a picture through story of what that looks like. Then make sure to share the story.

And remember, if you are not sharing stories, you are practicing *not sharing* stories. You will get good at not sharing. In the absence of a positive, nutritional story, a harmful, morale-killing story is sure to flood into that empty space. Create a piñata tradition: ritual ways of breaking open the good story basket with such enthusiasm that everyone is showered in the feel-good stuff. Games, competitions, creative projects. This is the kind of work culture that swallows stress and negativity whole, and leaves the community feeling served by light and hope.

STORY STRENGTHENS IMMUNE SYSTEMS

New workers are vulnerable to negative, traumatized stories from the tribe that greets them. This vulnerability is increased by false stories about their work that they inherited from social exposure and academic studies. They are also impressionable to healthy, positive tribal stories, which serve to strengthen their mental immune system for the challenges ahead. Our collection of healthy, hopeful, truthful stories makes up our immune system. We rely on this to manage stress and wellness.

This same attitudinal, spiritual immune system can be worn down and weakened in tenured workers who have been exposed to harmful work elements for years. For these workers, daily infusion of nutritious stories is valuable to maintain strength, spirit, and endurance. Years of work can also create a cataract that blinds workers to the beauty of their work and of coworkers and those they serve. Stories filled with vitality prevent and dissolve these cataracts, helping people see clearly the venerable nature of who they are and what they do.

PROTECT YOUR STORY

In this work, and in our group experience together, so many of our nutritious, healing stories get lost. We go down to the river each day, the river of a sacred moment shared with someone (service recipient, coworker, etc.), and we gather pure, refreshing water (inspired story). Then the day happens. Chaos, unpredictability, fatigue, distraction. As we journey through this wilderness, the water we gathered is steadily leaking, through our unwellness, out onto the ground. It evaporates and is lost forever. Our challenge is: *How do we get our pure water from the river all the way to the village (community or workplace) where we can share it with so many thirsty souls?* It is possible to deliver all our pure water, if we learn what story preservation means.

Your personal and group stories are precious. They determine the quality of your work experience. Make sure you protect them from harmful influences. People with destructive stories brewing inside will want to pour their story into yours, turning your inspirational story into a horror story. Put out false story fires quickly, before they spread. As a group or organization, protect your story by spending time examining and celebrating it. Insulate your story from high turnover rates by ensuring that you have storytellers in place who aren't going anywhere soon. And even if they do, make sure you have processes in place for the handing off of the story. Have a plan of succession for your story. Your culture resides in your story. Groups that maintain their culture over the years place a priority on story-keeping. When the media gets your tribe's story wrong, have the true story ready for reply. Put it out there proactively, in times of calm in-between crisis and chaos. Keep watering the ground of your community with your true story. Then people will recognize when the false stories start making the rounds.

RENOVATE YOUR STORY

When was the last time you examined your story? If your clothes need washing, and your home needs spring cleaning, certainly your story can use some attention, too. Stories decay and fall into disrepair just like houses do. Time, elements, and wear and tear break down stories. They lose their essential tension and integrity. Other people's stories pollute yours. Your system culture dilutes your story. The pain of those you care for can fragment and bruise your story if you are not mindful. Stories are eroded by seasonal changes: turnover, new leadership, laws, policies, and practices. Moving from position to position is jeopardy for your story. So, great, now we agree: Your story can use some work.

Story renovation addresses *language, content, structure, and spirit.* All four determine our internal message. And while we're at it, we might as well scrub away at our team or unit story, and our larger system story. We need to ask certain questions: *What am I telling myself about this work? Who do I say I am in this work? What am I saying is the point of this work? What worth or value do I recognize in this work?* The same questions apply to the collective. Honesty is required in answering these questions. We may not like some of the answers. Those are the ones that can offer us the most value. They reveal changes we need to make to our story. The answers that feel good, those are the ones we need to celebrate and appreciate. Let's make sure we give them the kind of home within our story that they preciously deserve.

Renovation is a matter of dedicating exclusive time to spend with our story: Personal reflection. Staff retreat. Agenda item for a staff meeting. Team or agency initiative. However creative we choose to be will determine the renovation methods at which we arrive. Renovation is a process of removing old paint (ideas), deconstructing broken furniture, walls, and flooring (relationships), and building and polishing a new narrative (home). There is no reason we can't have fun while we renovate. This is a creative act. It can even be a form of play. Pull things apart. Look at them from new angles. See if they really fit together. Be willing to reassemble the old arrangement into a new puzzle. Don't take it personally when pieces of the broken-down story get thrown out. Instead, take very personally your duty to put in new, helpful pieces.

A story is a living, breathing companion in our work. A cardiovascular system that determines atmosphere. It is so fluid that its shape and tone are altered virtually by the moment. Pay close attention when people, whether new workers or tenured ones, add new language and meaning to the story, especially to your personal story. You are the arbiter of your personal story. You get to decide what language to keep or reject. As a team or group, assume the same power. What you want is a story that works, that shines, that feels good, and fosters good work. Keep renovating until you get there. Then, make sure that even the ongoing renovation becomes a part of your story.

ANANSI'S WEB

Anansi the Spider is an important figure in African folklore. Emerging out of Asante culture of what is modern-day Ghana, Anansi is seen as the keeper of all stories. Anansi stories have been shared throughout the African diaspora for centuries and often symbolize a people's resistance to oppression and survival. Anansi worked hard to acquire all the stories of the land. He worked hard to keep them. As a result, African culture reveres the place of Story in the wellness of a people.

Every system, group, and person needs its stories. More to the point, each needs a way to gather, preserve, and share its healing and power stories, and to get rid of its toxic stories. All groups need their version of Anansi's Web. Some people are natural storytellers. Others are natural story recorders. All of these people need to be placed in roles that allow them to use this gift, this superpower, on behalf of the tribe. If your group can develop several Anansi weavers, you may discover you possess a tensile strength and resilience that vibrates beautifully in the light and catches all the stories you need.

DREAMCATCHER

Arising long ago out of Indigenous Ojibwe culture is the now popular *Dreamcatcher*. Ojibwe have traditional stories of Asibikaashi, the Spider Woman, who cared for the children and the people. As Ojibwe territory grew, and Asibikaashi could no longer reach all the children, grandmothers and mothers began to weave magical webs for the children. Unfortunately, the dreamcatcher has now become obscenely commercialized. You can see it dangling from plenty of car rearview mirrors. Its essence, though, is as a sacred instrument for preserving the interior landscape of a child's mind and spirit. For purifying and protecting children as they dream, and live. Historically, the dreamcatcher was positioned above the heads of children as they slept, to catch good dreams during the night and hold them for the children until morning. And to catch bad dreams, as an air filter might, so that those nightmares could be burned away by the sunrise.

Who are our dreamcatchers in our work? What system structures, processes, and traditions serve the role of dreamcatcher? This matters because every day, those who serve lives are experiencing daydreams and *daymares*. Beautiful, healing stories, and horrific, scarring stories. If we are not mindful, the good dreams evaporate in the climate of stress and neglect, while the bad dreams remain to be soaked in by workers and leadership over and again. This is how tragic events in a system are still being talked about 5 and 10 years later, as though they are still happening. Trauma needs a dreamcatcher. Each of us can be that sacred hoop.

THREE ATMOSPHERES OF WELLNESS

Three atmospheres of wellness exist for each of us: *The climate within ourselves, within our life space. The climate within the system of which we are a part. And the climate within our service relationships.* These three atmospheres are intimately interwoven. Culture and training have taught us to perceive and experience all things in parts, fragments, separation. The inescapable truth is that there is no separation. Our failure to realize this is at the root of our suffering. We believe that if we only improve our *engagement with families and communities,* this will somehow magically take away our need to face ourselves personally or within our agency space. We will do anything to avoid reckoning with personal change, the root of system change. Our federal and state laws reflect this avoidant behavior. Our policies, practices, and attitudes reflect this. We burn vast energy finding displaced focuses that feel more comfortable to us, then build entire funding cycles and service paradigms around these displaced, more convenient targets: *child-centered, community-based, culturally sensitive, cultural humility, diversity,* and on and on. But beyond these rhetorical feel-good notions, what about the difficult truth of our own inner ailments? Wellness is a labor in Love with its own interior lands.

THE NATURE OF TRAUMA

It is important that we understand the true nature of trauma, so that we can effectively prevent, identify, and address it within us, and within others. Although our common conception of trauma is that it is a pathology, its actual purpose is to protect us. It is a vestige of our primal wiring for survival. When we experience something harmful, our whole being—mind, body, heart, and spirit—records an imprint of that experience. Then, when we encounter that experience again, or even anticipate it, our system sets off an alarm, as if to say, "Don't go there again!" That alarm, or warning system, exists in the form of fear, anxiety, adrenaline, tension, constriction, defensiveness, increased prejudice, and an array of other psychological and physiological tools. This warning system is effective when helping us avoid what is harmful to us. A problem emerges, however, when we are unable to avoid these harmful triggers, and especially when we are exposed to them chronically.

A further jeopardy arrives when our trauma imprint overflows its original stimulus-response sensitivity and becomes generalized to other life stimuli. In this way, trauma is much like a bodyguard we have hired to keep us safe from the stalkers of modern life. And our bodyguard initially does a great job. Unfortunately, our bodyguard has aspirations not only to protect us, but also to become us! And so, with our every encounter with genuinely harmful life elements, our bodyguard is being exercised, growing stronger, more powerful. And more lustful. Let's say that your bodyguard's original assignment was to keep you away from physical harm. And it did. It was quick to jump into action when a large tree branch started to fall on you, or when a car was about to drift into your driving lane. But now, your bodyguard is intoxicated with the call to duty. It jumps into action when a twig blows toward you in the wind. Or, when you are simply on the road, driving. Just the presence of other cars is now enough to send your bodyguard into egotistic fervor. Trauma is insecure, always trying to prove itself to you. Proving that it is ready and willing to send you into panic at the slightest provocation. Or at no provocation at all.

Trauma rarely stays put in its place. Especially if we do not work to heal it. It is like a forest floor full of mushrooms, continuously growing and multiplying in optimal conditions of shade and moisture. Inattention to our trauma provides shade and moisture to feed its fungal nature. If we are not culling back its growth, it does not remain static. It grows. Trauma is a hosting of runaway ghosts, all clamoring to let us know just how much we have to fear and avoid in life. It becomes difficult for us to discern our true, healthy voice from the rambling of all those ghosts. Trauma is a greatly diversified virus. It exists as physiological activity. As physiological alteration. As mental and emotional conditioning. As psychological perception. As behavioral habit. This diversification makes trauma difficult to eradicate. And further, trauma, being habitual, is empowered each time it is activated. It is our personal chaperone run amok, scaring away all our potential dance partners: Joy, Peace, Security, Health, Clarity, Creativity, and the rest.

Trauma within us is like a baby. If we pay it attention, it will calm down. If we ignore it, it will scream piercingly until our every nerve is shot and shattered. And trauma is an off-duty firefighter convinced that the world is burning and needs its help to avoid certain destruction. Because this off-duty firefighter has a nature rooted in compassion, a desire to assist, it springs out of bed, throws on its clothes, and rushes out the door and into the fray. It may be missing a sock, or be unshaven and disheveled, but the firefighter will not be deterred. It shows up at the scene of your real-life moment and starts spraying everything down with adrenaline and fear. It takes an axe to your serenity, splintering all your structures that house Peace.

These are just some of the many faces of trauma. Only when we begin to understand trauma's persona, are we empowered to prevent, manage, and heal it.

VICARIOUS TRAUMA

All trauma is vicarious. So the term *vicarious trauma* is in some ways redundant. All trauma ends up in us by virtue of a social experience. Even hurt we cause ourselves is inherited from hurt others have caused us. Trauma is a relational artifact. What we see, hear, feel, learn, and are touched by through direct and indirect relationship feeds us or harms us. Some of the benefit or harm is a product of our perception, how we see the experience. And some of the benefit or harm is a function of objective nature. Either way, because we are such intensely social creatures, we are vulnerable to trauma, which uses social virulence as a carrier for its desire to spread.

Since trauma is vicarious by nature, we can treat trauma vicariously. If relationship caused a wound, relationship can be used to cure the wound. When a system values relationship over process and invests in putting the *social* in social servitude, it gives its people their best chance of learning how to stay healthy together. Relationship is used not only as influence but also as example. Gather your wild people who dare to be whole, healthy, positive, and kind, and send them on a courageous mission: Let them be in relationship with the rest of the tribe. Watch vicarious vitality do its work.

THE MOMENT PAIN ENTERS

In the very moment pain enters us, we tell ourselves a story about this pain. The story we tell is a function of our life experience and how we have chosen to make sense of that experience. This initial story acts as a moderating and mediating filter for the new pain during its moment of birth in us. The story morphs, contorts, disfigures, diminishes, or magnifies the actual pain into a product of our perception. When we tell a hurtful story about our new pain, we have entered into a deeper pact with suffering. It is not that we have not been legitimately wounded. It is that even our new wound has a wound. That wound is created by the story we tell. In our work, the stories we choose to tell ourselves about people, places, and moments shape our ability to do the work, and how the work affects us.

Ego, when activated in the wrong direction, amplifies pain. Compassion, when active, modifies pain—yet another reason that we benefit from practicing mindfulness with ego, and celebration of compassion. Our work involves pain. We know this. It is a part of the climate of human suffering. Knowing this, we prepare for the pain on its way, not by growing hard and closed, but by nurturing our compassion. Compassion becomes the way we welcome pain into our reality. Compassion provides us with a language for our nubile pain story that imbues this new pain with meaning and purpose. Compassion softens our way of receiving and making sense of the pain that arrives to us vicariously and personally.

The moment pain enters us is a vital moment. A birth moment. The care we take with a newborn baby serves as a helpful example of the kind of tenderness, attentiveness, softness that new pain requires. This is a skill. We care for the needs of others by learning how to care for how pain enters us. The more nurturing we are in these moments, the less damage pain does as it lives in us. And the more productive we become in using pain to bring meaning and motivation to our work reality. The first glance of pain can spasm us into closure. We can learn to respond by opening into the space that pain affords: the space of pure sensation and circumstance. Pain clarifies, if we let it. In clarity, we have a chance to proceed, creating new clarity together. Life is always sculpting us. So is our story, every time we are touched.

Let us be honest here. Do you hold onto your trauma as though it is a precious newborn baby, afraid to let anyone touch it, much less to offer a single idea for alleviating it? If so, do not be hard on yourself; you are far from alone. Trauma is a habit. As with all habits, we can loathe separation from our trauma, even if it does us harm. Yes, separation anxiety happens with our trauma, too. Identity is a powerful part of our existence, our sense of being. Whatever we tell ourselves we are, we tend to hold tightly onto that, no matter how detrimental that self-concept may be.

And this is how our trauma becomes woven into our garment of identity. Trauma starts with an experience. Even an inherited or vicarious one, passed on to us from someone who had the actual experience. This experience then becomes a part of the story we tell ourselves *about* ourselves. Soon, even the worst of traumas becomes, strangely, a badge of pride in the sense that we have a deep need to feel good about ourselves, no matter how low our actual self-regard.

And so we tell ourselves, and others, the story of our trauma. That story, with all its strands, becomes our security blanket, our way of affirming and validating our existence, and all the emotions, thoughts, and behaviors that come with it. Should anyone or anything come along that might possibly separate us from our trauma, and therefore from our concept of *Self*, we often react in apparently illogical ways. Trauma is a bruise we don't want anyone to touch. And yet, being caringly touched is a core part of healing. This is the great paradox of our trauma.

Think of the so-called *Bag Lady*. She is physically homeless, materially indigent, carrying with her all the things she considers her possessions. These may be kept in a shopping cart or in bags, and the items may have no real value to those who do not share her life condition. But the key is, these things are *hers*. In her mind, in her perception, these things are a part of her. They define her. They are her adapted mode of self-valuation. She can say to herself: *These things are mine. Therefore I am a worthy person, for I have worked hard to have these things. I take care of them*. If we come along, hoping to help her with her circumstance, one of our thoughts may be to help her release her *baggage*, so that she can focus on achieving *more valuable* things in life. And so, we attempt to help. But to her, we are now a danger. We have come for her *stuff.* So, she defends her stuff, her *Self,* with all her might. She may even grow violent. She believes that we are a threat to her survival.

We can react in very similar ways to any external presence we believe seeks to separate us from our trauma. That presence may be a person, a program or policy, a book or article, a leadership or culture change, or even an idea. Being ever so creative, we swiftly come up with many ways to resist this separation from our trauma. When faced with ideas that threaten our trauma bond, we say things like, "That idea sounds good in theory, but..." This is one of the hallmark signs of resistance to releasing our trauma. We devalue any idea as simply an idea, missing out on the reality that the idea may also exist and have been validated *in practice.*

We attack the source of the idea, saying, "I am dealing with stress and trauma that you cannot comprehend. No one understands the work I do. This idea may apply to others. Not to me. Not to my reality." Notice the territorial assertion of boundaries between *me* and *us,* and *you* and *them.* This drawing of lines is a classic way of shutting down any process that might result in separating us from our trauma or the trauma involved in our work. *Someone is trying to steal my stash! I've worked too hard for this! How can anyone or any idea reduce my trauma to something that can be taken from me?* It is as though we feel someone is distilling our own blood and siphoning it away from us. Loss of identity, and even transition of identity, can be this painful.

And so, we hoard our trauma. We believe it is more comfortable to endure the suffering created by our trauma and vicarious trauma, than to risk the unknown of learning new ways of being. Even if those new ways of thinking, interpreting, feeling, and acting allow us to heal, renew our optimal wellness, and empower our capacity to serve other lives. We hoard our trauma with subtle mind games, and slick avoidance tactics. We hoard until our trauma piles so high within our being that we cannot breathe, cannot see clearly, cannot function. We hoard ourselves all the way to burnout, fatigue, disillusion, depression, ill health, and even death. This is how dearly we can hold on to our trauma. Understanding this is a first step on the road to knowing how to more productively use trauma, and when to let our old "friend" go.

LETTING TRAUMA GO

Trauma tends to cling to us and try to keep us close. It becomes a quicksand pit into which we fall. From there, we keep telling trauma's story even if life has moved on and it is days, months, or years in the future. It takes conscious determination for us to begin telling a new story. Personally and together, we need to catch each other and support our new story.

Any letting go can create sadness and anxiety. Even the thought of letting go. Our letting-go acts would appreciate ceremony. Ceremony is the security blanket wrapped around the heart, mind, and spirit that says, "Sushhh, now. It's going to be alright." Since we come to view our trauma as a part of us as much as a bone or organ, and even as a friend, we really could use ceremony and social support to let trauma go. This isn't to say we can't do it on our own. It's just that support, encouragement, and witnessing can do wonders.

By ceremony, I don't mean grandiose décor and behavior, although by all means if you're feeling it, go for it. Instead, I mean ceremony as an act of mindfully moving through an experience by highlighting meaning and purpose along the way. This highlighting comes to reside in our memory where it exerts an echo through the spirit, reminding us that we are new. We forget we are new, all the time. Identity is a habit. We fall back into it the moment our new habit weakens. Ceremony takes new identity to the gym and trains it for the new life ahead. And ceremony shouldn't be a one-time thing. Letting trauma go happens in waves and layers and circles. It is not a linear language. It speaks in subtleties, sand grains that shuffle in the night and become new dunes. Ceremony then, needs to be ongoing. It is a chaperone for letting go.

USING TRAUMA

When we are traumatized, we are very sensitive to anything that even looks like it relates to our trauma. We can view this tendency as a negative, or as an opportunity. When we place ourselves, or are placed, in positions where we can use our trauma passion to advocate for new ways of doing things, we are super-powered. The celebrated historical figures who led change did so fueled by a passionate response to what had harmed them so deeply. When we view a person's trauma through the prism of a narrow present moment, without context or purpose, we may judge her or his trauma and resent the person. If we pull back and see the larger landscape, we may see that ahead on the road are places where we can use the passion this person's trauma has created. Revolutionaries succeed because of their trauma, not in spite of it.

TRAUMA SENSITIVITY

Many organizations strive to be *trauma-informed*. But being informed does not assure that a workforce will activate that information, or that the collective culture will become *trauma-sensitive*. It is this culture of sensitivity toward which we should set our sights. Workers and leaders should see themselves as the most effective, reliable, practical tool for creating and maintaining a trauma-sensitive workplace. Recognizing trauma in yourself, your colleagues, and your staff is a matter of being familiar with what trauma looks like, then caring enough to see it. Acting to prevent or minimize it is even better.

A trauma-sensitive organization can be recognized by certain traits. In such environments we find a clear awareness of and sensitivity to the nature of trauma in people, families, staff, and leadership. And an awareness of the role of mutual care in moderating and mediating the effects of trauma. These organizations effectively prevent trauma from escalating to counterproductive levels, in all sectors, and on all levels of authority. They possess a capacity to proactively address the effects of trauma in those they serve, and in staff and leadership.

These workforces feel safe and encouraged to contribute their unique gifts and skills to the work. They feel empowered, validated, supported, and celebrated. Not periodically or on calendar dates, but intrinsically, daily. Such agencies carry a strong culture of relationship investment and development. They have an internalized, ritualized habit of compassionate response to trauma, stress, and crisis; and a strong value of wellness, self-care, and mutual care. A trauma-sensitive organization practices what it preaches, in a very real sense. Its climate is a manifestation of its stated values. Its relationships thrive, and rather than being impediments in the work and sources of conflict, they are precious resources for service delivery, and a means of resolution for social and vocational challenges. Trauma sensitivity implies not only a reactive quality, but also a proactive one. A tuning into, preparation for, and action on behalf of not only managing trauma, but also healing it, first of all in those who do the work.

OCEAN IN A JAR

If we do not become better at releasing our soul through the pure emotion of feeling, crying, and tears, we become the ocean cramming itself into a jar. There can be no hope for such a jar (our body), straining to hold the immensity. Glass does not bend, it shatters. This is the fate of those who suppress their emotion. Ocean has no hope forced inside a jar. It cannot complete its work that way, reduced and bottled. Ocean has one way: consume and drown the jar so the jar becomes ocean. Order your emotional strategy. Now destroy your order. Imagine what it feels like for the jar, swallowing and hoarding an elephant into its glass acorn. *Live* the feeling ocean feels: its enormity stuffed impossibly. You jumping into a thimble. *Feel* the acute abrasion.

The house you are has openings. Use them. Water surges inside your plumbing. Tap that pressure before your pipes cry *Uncle*. Emotional outpouring is the rush of a garden hose in summer. You know the outcome for the grass, those human blades who are your brown parched lawn of social world. This is a matter of what you owe the baker who made you as bread. Your rising would be a start. Be a child who leans over an old well in day's heat looking for something cool and clear. Give up your illusory balance that only keeps you still unnaturally, a straightjacketed soul. Instead, fall in the well and stay there. Learn to weep like its damp walls and satisfy your thirst internally. Become a pupil, a glass jar who drowns in the ocean. An amnesiac who completely forgets how to hold things in. This may be the opposite of what your workplace teaches you to be. Be it anyway.

EMOTIONAL TERRAIN OF AN ORGANIZATION

Organizations that serve people in crisis and need are places of great emotional sensitivity. Trauma is traveling throughout workers and workplaces, creating an ever-changing emotional topography. This requires leaders and workers who are adept at reading and responding to the terrain. This is the actual foundation of healing work. Not the processing of cases, which comes to seem like a mountainous priority. No, not that. Managing stress, anxiety, and emotions must be an organizational priority, for it is within this daily stream that the process work gets done, not done, well done, or poorly done. Outcomes are determined not most of all by technical skill, but by wellness skill. Healthy, fruitful organizations, workers, and leaders embrace this truth. They find a zest for being in tune with mood, tenor, and spirit.

It is no longer acceptable not to be a *people person*. Every person is capable of being a people person in this healing work. Whether introverted, shy, insecure, or socially privileged, people on every authority level can be held accountable for, and practice, caring about their impact and relationships. We do not exist in offices and cubicles, in meeting rooms or in the field. This is an illusion. We exist inside thoughts and emotions. Tuning into each other empowers us to be assessors and practitioners of emotional terrain, the land where we humans most truly exist.

FUEL GAUGES

Personally and as groups, we need to develop internal fuel gauges. Ways of being in touch with our critical levels. When our morale, energy, spirit, or sense of purpose lag, we need to have a reliable way of recognizing this. Daily assessment is helpful, especially when we do it in quick, fun, creative ways. Talk to yourself. Don't worry about being perceived as crazy. You are crazy. Or you wouldn't be doing this work. Journal, create lists, use your relationships therapeutically. I don't mean to vent your issues onto everyone. I mean, in your regular conversations, talk about how you are doing, listen to how others are doing, feed each other. You know how schools have hallway or playground monitors? Choose people at work to be your wellness monitors. Invite them to be real with you by letting you know when they notice something is off. Be a wellness monitor for others. Being attentive to their wellness tunes you into your own. *Fuel gauges.* We need more of them, and we need to keep them tuned.

PERCEPTION IS REALITY

For human beings, what we perceive to be real is, in effect, real. Objective reality matters very little. We are subjective creatures. We create and inhabit subjective worlds. This makes communication and relationship even more vital. It is not enough to feed people statistics and plans and expect them to believe in change. They must be provided continuous opportunities to witness, feel, touch, smell, and hear change. We all need evidence that we can feed into our subjective machinery. And we need our coworkers and leaders to validate our subjective perception. This is why acknowledgement is nonnegotiable. If people's sense of reality is not acknowledged, validated, they will either lose faith in themselves or in their system. Or, very often, both.

Appearance matters because what something appears to be is how it is likely to be perceived, regardless of the truth. Executive leadership needs to be very sensitive to how actions, decisions, words, and behaviors (or the absence of each of these) appear to workers. Workers need to be sensitive to the very same things coming from them: the appearance of their persona. In a mutually caring environment, people care about the appearance of things. Communication is nurtured to minimize misunderstanding. Strong relationships lessen the occurrence of harmful, inaccurate perceptions by hosting vibrant communication and sharing. Care is taken to habitually explore appearance and reality.

MEANING AND PURPOSE

Meaning and purpose are the air we breathe to stay vital. Modern culture is drained of both. In their places, illusion, distraction, and hollow comfort are celebrated. Without meaning and purpose in our life and work, meaning that aligns with our nature and calling, we are as trees without roots, plants without sun. We gradually suffocate, wither, and die. Some, through sheer will or stubbornness, keep going on in the workplace even long after they have died. These are the zombie kind. Let us not mock them, for in one way or another, they are most of us. How do we know this? Our culture, void of meaning and purpose, is the ecology and atmosphere from which each of us draws. Therefore, if we claim *zombiehood* as our common culture, we can also say this is our own socio-nutritional state: high calorie, low meaning and purpose. Bones break this way. Diseases break out. We endure, but deflated, running on fumes.

One of our wellness objectives can be stated concisely: *Always connect to purpose.* In everything that we do and say, we make sure to connect it to purpose. That is how we stay home inside our true calling. When we are not able to daily gather clear, purposeful meaning from our work, we lose our sense of nobility, and fall into monotony. This harms everyone. Humans need to feel noble in the same way that parents need to feel like parents. That is, we thrive on our contribution to the common cause. Groups that discuss the richness and absence of nobility in their work atmosphere are better able to create cultures that foster nobility. What we talk about, we activate. Monotony grows in places (hearts, offices) where monotony is the language. As with stones or weeds in our garden, we need to remove monotony, too.

Reinstituting meaning and purpose is largely a matter of ceremony and ritual. And of examination. For a personal transfusion, to get our blood vital again, we can choose to pause and examine our lives. Whatever we find, we begin to sort into piles: healthy over here, unhealthy over there. At this point, we have prepared for *ceremony and ritual.* These two structures can be created or reclaimed from our own life. They exist, either latent or discarded, in our past wellness, our visions of the future, and in the practices of others we know. In other words, we do not need to wait for someone to give us ceremony and ritual. We can be students and learn, but the essence of both is observation. Being present. Summoning meaning. A strong enough sense of meaning is fertile ground for purpose to emerge. Purpose, once flowered, becomes a good host for meaning. Symbiosis. To bring more meaning and fulfillment into your personal and collective work experience, join whatever soulful stream is running at the moment. If people are laughing, allow yourself to laugh. When people cry, feel free to cry with them, not in despair, in communion, because you Love them. And you are one of them.

PRACTICE MODELS

Funny thing about practice models. You have to practice them. I have seen countless counties and states invest for years in practice models, only to yield so-so results. These initiatives tend to focus heavily on information dissemination, while neglecting the role of process and the psychology of practice. Often, this is because leadership fails to involve the guidance of people gifted in facilitating *process*. The literature on learning and growth is clear: We humans are not machines that simply synthesize information. We require soulfulness, a sense of meaning and purpose to what we are supposed to learn. If information, and its delivery mode, do not stir and awaken us, we are not as likely to internalize the lesson.

For practice models to become manifest as system culture, people need the process to feel as though it has emerged out of them, not that it has been imposed upon them. This is why process needs to be paid significant attention. A sense of ownership is critical, or people won't be emotionally invested in practicing. Without earnest, long-term practice, we can never know whether the principles of our model hold true in real-life work and service relationships. We abandon the practice model without ever having given it a fair chance to breathe and condense.

For people to feel that a model is from them, about them, and for them, ideally they need to be a part of the visioning and strategizing. We're talking about community members and workforces here, not just an exclusive set of leadership. This kind of inclusiveness rarely occurs early in the process. But it is always helpful to include the masses, even if late in the game. Otherwise, the precious buy-in that leaders seek for their system change models does not materialize. The whole enterprise is seen as just another condescending rollout of political and fiscal priority that isn't in the interest of communities or workers. And so, any practice model that has to do with healing and humanizing work and service relationships, needs to be grounded in... you guessed it (or maybe you didn't): relationships. The psychology of change dictates that if you want me to take on something as my own, then you need to interact with me in honoring, horizontal, mutual relationship even as you begin visioning and planning the process. Let my needs and realities as a worker or community member shape the nature and ongoing course of the initiative. If you are *real* with me, I might *really* practice the practice model.

THREE HEALTHY CHOICES

When faced with a reality that does not feel good to us, we can respond in one of three healthy ways: *We can work to change the situation, we can find peace within the situation, or we can leave the situation.* Commonly, we stay in the situation and complain about it, making no real effort and taking no true accountability for our role in changing our reality. This is what we see in dysfunctional, traumatized workplaces: Festering. Acute anger and resentment. Blame and villainizing. At some point along the way, people give up on all three healthy options, dig in, and pitch a fit. This is understandable. It is not helpful. In fact, it is entirely destructive for the person and group.

To counter this tendency, work together to keep your group on track. You have a mission to accomplish. All efforts should be in the direction of wellness and peace. You are either going to give all you have, indefinitely, to changing your work reality, or you are going to give all you have, indefinitely, to finding peace within your reality. Ideally you will do both. And sometimes, it is meant for us to leave the situation—our team, unit, department, or organization. Everything has its season. Except the willful detonation of your colleague's wellbeing, the poisoning of everyone's water because of your own suffering. Again, this is understandable. It is never excusable. The work is already hard enough for everyone. So, keep your eyes on the prize: change, peace, and/or release. These choices are one way to care for yourself and those who serve by your side.

THE PSYCHOLOGY OF CHANGE

As people and groups, we tend to focus heavily on our desired change outcomes. And on our modes of change. Often we neglect the root of both outcome and mode: *the psychology of change*. If we do not pay attention to the psychology, we are likely to fall short of our potential for lasting, impactful transformation.

We will fight change to the death. Literally. But even on a more benign level, what about the worker who refuses an adjustment that will improve his work experience or outcomes? The supervisor or manager who will not budge from her way of doing a relatively small thing? We protest change repeatedly: "Who moved my chair?" "Why do we have to switch our staff meeting time?" "I always sit in that seat at these meetings." We are like superglue, adhered with a vengeance to our trivial and even harmful habits. Treating anyone who points this out as a threat worthy of scorn. To dislodge us from this, information is not enough. We also need an infusion of meaning that sparks our deeper motive.

BELIEF IS THE ROOT OF CHANGE

If we do not believe something is possible, we will not give ourselves to it. This is a primal design in our nature, meant to help us survive by not allocating resources (attention, energy, memory, effort) to something that will not bear fruit. Our work and workplaces, when ailing, suffer from a drought of faith. Faith, the evidence of things unseen. Ground of hopefulness. What our true, clarified vision beholds beyond today.

Organizations strive over and again to change themselves without ever examining and nurturing internal belief in that change. Faith has roots: We must be clear as to what the change is. Where it leads. What its point is. We must be assured that what we contribute or invest will pay benefits, that there will be reward. And it helps to know that our group cannot change without us. Without our effort and brilliance.

People who have belief need to be placed in roles within the change process that allow them to spread their faith. Even better, they can be invited to choose these roles. If they have belief, they will be natural leaders for the cause. I have seen the most faithless become the most dominant voice in their resistance to change. Where is the storytelling strategy to minimize the impact of the doubters and position the voice of the faithful? Faith is a seed and must be watered. Having a blueprint for change, a magical practice model, is not enough. Who is doing the watering? Who is the sunlight? And who is the fertile soil?

FEARING CHANGE

If you wish to help yourself or others budge from a paralyzing fear of change, try to shift the focus to an even greater fear. Fear of losing your job? That's always a winner. If people feel they can go on doing their work in harmful ways without losing their job, they just might. Go on, that is. *Why not*, they ask. We can become much better at connecting the dots between dysfunction, unwellness, new cultures and standards, and the idea of losing your job. This may sound cruel. But motivating truth is a kindness even if it cuts. Other great fears can be used: Fear of dying. It is not a far leap between poor health and dying. Fear of group rejection. This is another powerful motivator. Strong cultures make clear to every worker, new and tenured, that certain ways will not be tolerated, and the absence of certain ways also will not be tolerated. Demonstrated consequence does wonders to motivate change.

Deep caring also helps massage people through their fear of change. Rather than flood people with bureaucratic dictates and ultimatums, change requirements can be conveyed through real relationship in a way that feels caring. Think about how you would want someone to tell you that you need to change. Whatever you come up with can be your template for nurturing others through their fear. Also, the more groups talk supportively about their various fears, while exploring actionable resolutions and supports, the more that fear evaporates. Fear really only lives inside humans and in the atmosphere of fearful groups. Once it has been released into a strong, faithful environment, it fades away.

BEING NEW

A big part of caring, helping work is about being new. New to our role and responsibility. New to always changing laws, policies, practices, and personalities. New to the community and its cultures. New to the current social epidemics. Some of us pitch fits and rail against having to be new in any aspect of our work. But isn't enduring newness what we ask of children and adults of foster care, homelessness, incarceration, mental health challenges, physical illness, learning challenges, school and neighborhood migration, poverty, linguistic dislocation, and trauma? Do we not ask them to bravely endure all their newness, with open hearts and minds and a positive attitude? Systems, workers, and leaders should be a resonant example of how to be new in a way that is healthy. Our work conditions constantly change. This is hard. But we also get to practice being new, and then share that sensitivity with all the people we care for, who are journeying through their own reality of being new. An old word is true: *A certain grace comes with being new.*

USE THE RIGHT CHANGE TOOLS

Systems tend to fall in love with rhetoric and policy when facing a need to change. But only behavior and attitudes determine climate and culture, not rhetoric and policy. Rhetoric is a drunken language. When we use it, we ourselves end up hungover. We realize after the fact that rhetoric is empty of meaning, and only meaning gives change real roots. In order for the language we use with ourselves and each other to carry the nutrient of meaning, it must be language nested in ongoing behavior and attitude practice. This is why all the trainings in the world will make little difference, if a person, group, or service tribe is not invested in authentic behavior and attitude projects.

Tell a young child that because of the daylight savings clock change in spring that it is time for bed, and the child will look out the window and see it is still light outside. The child will not believe that it is time for bed. For a child, darkness and light are real. Time change is only an idea. For people, behaviors and attitudes are real. We will not believe a change is happening just because rhetoric and policy say so. Only behaviors and attitudes can convince us.

As for policy, change does not respond to policy as much as it sneers at it. This does not mean that policy is not important for system change. It is vital. But policy too often is thrown out into dysfunction as though it is an independent cure. This is like throwing a rulebook to a group of fighting rhinos and expecting them to make peace. First of all, as far as we know, rhinos can't read. Secondly, dysfunction does not respond to rules. It responds to relationship. To the insistent influence of healthful social behavior and attitudes. Once a system makes relational wellness the core of its work, the improving relationships act as a tonic against dysfunction. It is within this context that policy is then able to affirm and fortify a culture.

CREATE OPENNESS TO CHANGE

We human beings are notoriously resistant to change. We will often work harder at not changing than we would have had to work to change. Part of this is fear of the unknown. But an underestimated factor is that we simply dislike letting go of old habits and familiarities, even if they are harmful. To help open people to change, we (and they) need to address and manage their fears and stresses, and they need to be shown clearly how they and the group will benefit from the proposed changes.

Asking staff for what changes they recommend is a first step in gaining their trust and sense of ownership over the change to come. A sure way to spark an angry revolution is to impose change, even if that revolution remains an inward simmering of souls. If you are a worker or a liaison (mid-level) leader, teach upward in a caring way. Let your executive management understand: "This is what our people need." And how do you know this? Because they have said so, and their say so is your direction to go.

The language and tone we choose when messaging staff is vital. Especially with a change initiative. If your voice and words sound unsure and uninspired when communicating a change in law, policy, program, or practice, your staff will be influenced more by your language and tone than by the concept you share. Do you believe in the change for which you are advocating? If not, staff will sense it. Leaders often focus more on a vision than on tapping into their streams of inspiration, passion, and purpose. These streams soak the words and tone of leaders with sincerity and belief. This is what stirs a work tribe into courageous change.

Clarify the personal and group benefits of the proposed change. Children and adults like to understand *the why* of change. Encourage personal ownership of the change. Encouragement doesn't happen simply because we say, "Be encouraged." It is an organic thing that grows in people because we have given them power and influence in the process. Consistently and in a timely fashion, celebrate and reward personal and group change efforts. Provide personal and group time and space for reflection on the change. Allow safe space for expression of change-related questions and stresses. Invite and welcome feedback in an inclusive fashion. Regularly status-check on both the personal and group level, and course-correct when necessary. Identify and promote superordinate goals (group goals that can only be reached via the contribution of each individual).

Work together to create conditions in which each person feels she or he has equal social power within the change process. Promote positive stories related to the change process. Collectively douse fires of negative storytelling rooted in the past. Minimize general stress. People open to change the more they are relaxed. Utilize small support teams to encourage each other through the change process. Allow for healthy grieving of lost habits, processes, and traditions. Celebrate the birth of new habits, processes, and traditions.

CARING

A prime ingredient in any relational space is caring. We don't have to know each other well, or even like each other. But we must care. And this caring must be mutual. It must extend in both directions across authority lines. A caseworker is responsible for caring for the needs and wellness of her supervisor, and vice versa. The same is true between supervisors and managers. Between associate directors and directors. In other words, relational spaces are nonhierarchical in nature. No caste systems apply.

Caring is motivational. It requires a sincere motive to support the needs and wellness of another. *Caring is attentional.* The motive to support should naturally manifest as genuine attention to the signs and signals that another is communicating, and to the circumstances and conditions in which that other person exists. Even if those conditions are beyond that person's awareness. *Caring is active.* Motive and attention should lead to action on behalf of the other person's needs and wellness. *Caring is receptive.* It is more motivated to receive from another (insight, sincerity, story, perspective, expression) than it is to dictate. When these qualities are present, then hurt, stress, fear, and dysfunction can be dissolved to a significant degree. Growing professionally requires technical skill. Relational skill is the best practice that gives technique its wings.

COMPASSION

Compassion is a highly popular word and greatly undervalued practice. We misunderstand its meaning, so we trivialize its power. Compassion is not kindness, sweetness, softness. It is a professional capacity arrived at through daily hard work. A determination to *feel* another's life, and out of that feeling to harvest understanding, perspective, insight, and something world changing that we might call... *relationship.* Filling out forms and completing tasks is not the work. Staying vulnerable, humble, open, attentive, curious, caring, and present *despite* the conditions... this is the work. Love and Compassion are the two hands of a Divine masseuse who can nurture away any worldly pain. In any moment, you can be that masseuse. Just care deeply. No matter what. If we care that our expertise, systems, services, and resources make any difference at all in human lives, then we have no choice but to practice and perform compassion.

COMPASSION BENEFITS

We are used to considering employment benefits monetarily. As we evolve socially, wellness and quality of life benefits are becoming more prized. Compassion is one of these work benefits.

One that each team member can choose to allocate to the collective pot, with no annual cap.

Compassion is a decided underdog in a traumatized society or system. Trauma isn't just an internal state. It is a culture. Trauma work culture confers value upon individualism, *fight or flight* mentalities, *every person for herself* attitudes, clannishness, and conflict. Trauma culture surely does not encourage compassion. And yet, endless research shows compassion, both shared and received, yields the very things that you as a social servant, and your system, desperately need. Compassion strengthens the actual immune system of both the giver and receiver. It decreases physiological, mental, and emotional pain. Compassion leads to less exhaustion and absenteeism in work; and greater commitment, investment, and teamwork. It improves our quality of life.

Compassion also leads to decreased stress, deeper calm, better coping, and to lower blood pressure and inflammatory cortisol levels. Compassion increases our ability to receive and give social support. It strengthens bonds, and the sense of belonging and purpose, while discouraging unhealthy behaviors including anger and conflict. And neurologically, we experience equal levels of pleasure whether engaging in compassion or receiving a reward.

It would seem that compassion would be a root value for workers, leaders, and systems. Instead, the concept is ridiculed, devalued, and not taken seriously in this *serious business* of serving human lives. We view compassion as a cute delicacy that is ancillary to our real work. I cannot tell you how many times I have heard professionals express contempt for focusing on kindness, compassion, and caring, while wanting nothing more than to get back to the *real work*. Clearly, we have all been conditioned into a fallacy about the essence of serving human lives. This essence surely does not include paperwork, quotas, and statistics, which are each supposed to be but tools. Tools for empowered by our compassion to manifest effectively in human lives. If we as healers do not realize this, or have forgotten this, no wonder decade after decade statistics on certain communities do not improve and often worsen. Perhaps we can benefit from a remedial lesson in what it means to be present in crisis. And just maybe a better definition of *the real work* awaits our enlightenment.

COMPASSIONATE LEADERSHIP

Compassionate leadership is by its very nature communal. It does not hoard power, it disseminates it. It does not seek control, it seeks harmony. It believes that leadership is a spirit dwelling in every soul, throughout the entire workforce, and that compassion is the fire that sets it free. Further, compassionate leadership is alive. Activated leadership is a spark that takes ideas and rhetoric and uses them as kindling to set your agency ablaze. Latent leadership is laden with fear and insecurity, never rustling from its sleep. It drags a tribe down. Activated leadership is an ideal on fire, branding each person with its persona. We know leadership is activated by how it feels when we come to work. The atmosphere is alive in a way that makes us want to breathe it.

Compassionate leadership is not a style. It is a state of being. This means it is a state that can be arrived at by anyone. *Style* implies something you try on for fit and suitability. A *state* is a capacity arrived at through personal investment and practice. This is why a focus on leadership styles leads to inauthentic fads and flashes of impact. People can read authenticity, and its absence. With compassionate leadership, we have arrived at a place of wellness, having tapped our ability to engage with an open heart and mind. We have grown calm and centered enough for humility, and to learn, listen, intuit, and trust. Compassionate Leadership is not a form of being soft, easy, or laissez faire. It is entirely solid, fortified, and fierce. Its fierceness lies in its determination to be well in relationship to ourselves and others. To be aware, open, and available. For this way of being, we need to have faith in the power of caring. And if we do not, we may need to examine our choice to be a part of the caring profession.

It is time to move away from system models that affirm monopolies of power. Social and operational power disseminated into the hands of each worker-leader dilates the cardiovascular system of an agency, flushes out social toxins, and empowers the workforce. Organizational attitude is a reflection of *leadership*. Executive, formal leadership and personal leadership. We are all leading each other into the attitudes we assume. Attitudes are not accidental or magical, they are consequential. They originate somewhere. Someone carries them forward. Search your various leadership streams. Where you find the culprits, instead of rallying a lynch mob, rally compassionate embrace of new leadership modes and attitudes.

COMPASSIONATE LISTENING

Honoring what someone else shares with us, and the sharing itself, can be called *Compassionate Listening*. This is not just an auditory effort. It involves tuning into people with all of your senses. It requires that we make an effort not to judge, presume, punish, or discourage what is being shared with us. All we need to do is be sincerely present, attentive, and caring. This by itself can create healing and a sense of support in the one who shares. It strengthens bonds and trust. When you listen because you care to, not because you have to, you are in the neighborhood of compassionate listening. Compassionate listening is a potent, curative best practice. A form of actual service delivery. How many times have you or people in your life said, "I just need someone to listen?"

One of the greatest healing powers we have is simply to listen compassionately when another person chooses to share with us. This healing, primarily, is not theirs. It is our own. Each time we activate our own compassionate nature as we intentionally receive what another shares, we are exercising and stretching our own capacity for compassion, and for receiving suffering in a way that transforms suffering itself. Compassion is a muscle. Picture it as the mouth and throat of a large baleen whale. As a calf, the whale practices what it sees its mother doing: opening her mouth wide, stretching her jaws, and dilating her throat to its limit. All so that she can take in the maximum amount of sea water and, therefore, the maximum amount of phytoplankton food that is her sustenance. The whale calf learns this behavior, even beyond its innate nature. As it grows, it repeatedly opens its mouth and throat to full extension, taking in larger amounts of water and food, becoming more capable of feeding and sustaining itself by virtue of repeated opening.

Compassion works like this in a human being. The more we practice opening our caring heart, the more our dilation muscle grows and strengthens. This also leaves us vulnerable in a world where we are often surrounded by the apparent opposite of caring. Without role models to inspire our practice of compassion, we can grow negligent. Our compassion muscle atrophies. We starve, for compassion is our own food, not just food we provide to others. For many of us, this atrophying occurs as a function of our journey from childhood to adulthood. Where once we may have cared intensely and without judgment for the smallest flower or insect, or for a suffering soul, now perhaps our compassion valve is clogged and crusted from endless layers of stress, damage, and delusions that come from the world around us. And the world within us.

This withering of our compassion muscle can directly impact our ability to support and serve the lives of others. In most human encounters, what others need most from us, regardless of our training, titles, or experience, is our compassion. Our caring, without judgment, for their reality and their rightful existence within the unique conditions of their own life. When supporting others professionally, we struggle with our urge to provide information. To dictate. After all, how else are we to validate our job and paycheck than by contributing knowledge and insight? Compassion, though, operates according to another dynamic: *receiving*. Receiving in a manner that elicits the healing capacity in the one who is sharing. Receiving in a way that creates a relational space that feels safe to the sharer.

Compassionate listening resists the urge to correct. It invests in *feeling* the other person, in order to manifest understanding. Compassionate listening is active and reflective. Active in that you are participating with your full attention. Reflective in that you are receiving the other person's expression sacredly, by opening up and learning, growing even in the moment. And this is always a powerful tool: Say, "Okay, this is what I heard you say. Please correct me if I am wrong." By saying this and meaning it, you show that you have been listening, and that your absolute priority is to understand what has been shared.

Compassionate listening is not fixated on gathering information. Instead, it is invested in summoning its own potential for caring. Caring, free of judgment, that taps our innate sensitivity, understanding, and empathy. Compassionate listening is not sympathetic or pitying. It is not territorial or strategic. Not manipulative or dishonest. Compassionate listening is a human characteristic arrived at through diligent work, until it becomes a professional skill and asset. It requires devoted work at learning to honor others by *feeling* their lives. And like the baleen whale, with each healthy feeling, we are able to take in more feeling.

We are each ocean harbors into which suffering souls seek to sail, so that they can find respite, restoration, and renewal. If we as harbors are filled with the silt of self-importance, condescension, or prejudice, then no matter how wonderful our bag of *best practices*, we are among the impeding factors that keep the suffering from reaching the port of wellness and stability to which they are indelibly entitled. So, how do we keep our harbor clear of silt and sediment? Continuous work at qualities such as gratitude, quietude, grace, humility, reverence, and honor. These qualities are not easily measured empirically, causing our system and society cultures to devalue them in the arenas of supporting children, families, and communities. These qualities also cannot be faked. Persons who open and share with us know quickly the degree of our sincerity. They either feel they are safe sharing with us, that we care; or they feel we are another one of caring's imposters, only pretending to listen so that we will know how to judge, label, categorize, corral, and track them.

We are often insecure as we listen. We believe the moment is for us to prove our qualifications, to respond with colonial imposition. Compassionate listening cures our own insecurity by allowing us to discover the infinite volume of our ability to listen with care, such that healing is inspired in us, and in the one to whom we listen. Compassionate listening then, is ultimate transformative tonic. And well worth the practice.

LOVING SPEECH

No matter what we have to say or write, we can do so in a tone and spirit that is gentle, tender, sensitive, honoring, and caring. When we do this, our very communication becomes a healing ointment and creates safe relationship spaces. There is no such thing as neutral speech. Our speech is either Loving or it is non-Loving. When it is non-Loving, it can do damage, whether or not we intend it. Loving speech is not baby talk, cooing, or fawning, though if you are feeling it, go for it. No, Loving speech is mindful of its power to create harm or benefit others. It chooses to be an ointment for the listener's tenderness, doubt, and fear. Loving speech builds safe spaces and relationships. It reassures, welcomes, invites, calms, nurtures, and inspires. It is not manipulative, but arises from a place of true sincerity. Loving speech cares about the other person. Imagine if every time you spoke, you beautified your world. Such a thing need not be a dream.

SOCIAL ILLNESS

I have received countless requests to address workforces on issues of race and culture. The topical language presented to me is usually tied to current funding streams and social trends, socially comfortable language not intended to directly acknowledge the pathology so prevalent in our society, but to skirt around the perimeter of the illness. I view this as a measure of tending to guilt and conflict without having the will to speak the truth of who we are. I am asked to speak on *cultural sensitivity, cultural awareness, cultural humility*... whatever is the current iteration of vague, avoidant language that only hints at our deep problem with the way certain human beings have always been treated by society and its systems.

But no amount of learning about other cultures is going to change people's deeply rooted prejudice, bigotry, and supremacy. These are true social illnesses. Ailments that putrefy the spirit and damage a person's ability to relate to other human beings as human, to convey oneself as a full human being, defined as one capable of living in harmony and honor with others. Not defining prejudice, bigotry, and supremacy as illnesses causes us not to act with acute urgency or seek healing. Instead, we pretend that trainings, information sharing, will somehow magically make this most uncomfortable reality go away. They don't. They aren't. They won't.

We cannot afford to have workers and leaders polluted with acute prejudice toward the people they serve. Nor can we permit our laws, policies, practices, and perspectives to remain poisoned by these most destructive social illnesses. By choosing to be passive and avoiding this painful truth and healing journey, we are willfully bringing people's social illness into contact with children, adults, and families in crisis and dysfunction. When crisis and dysfunction in people needing service encounter prejudice and supremacy in professionals, further trauma is bound to occur. When it does, communities and families don't heal, because they are still being assaulted by the same societal antipathy, devaluation, and dehumanization.

We pretend that poverty is the root cause of people's suffering because poverty doesn't implicate us on a personal or system level. Blaming poverty allows us to say it is communities that are flawed, that the people in them need to better themselves. Blaming poverty affords us not having to say, *I am a part of the problem. I need to change.* And so we gravitate toward comfortable suspects, like poverty. But poverty doesn't assault people, incarcerate them, poison them, beat them down, drug them, expel them from school, block them from housing and employment, make them feel unsafe, or treat them as less than human. Poverty does not perform genocide. Humans do that. Specifically, humans who are not well. And in this trauma-exposed work we do, we as professionals are at great risk of not being well.

Cultural humility is the latest of many funding stream trends. This makes it a fashionable topic that will come and go, like the others. But for culturally oppressed and dehumanized people, cultural humility is a prayerful demand. A demand that systems stop desecrating our sacredness. True humility has little to do with learning about other cultures, and everything to do with self-reckoning. It is a convicted, tireless, brave examination of the soul, forever asking the question: *How are we participating in this long genocide of people and their ways?*

True humility acknowledges the generational damage of cultural supremacy, the ongoing arrogance of its mentality and approaches. It sheds its control impulse and opens organically into relationship. True humility lets its spirit be broken. Not in paralyzing guilt, but in a conviction of justice and repair. True humility does not put the subject on a fiscal calendar. It plants the priority firmly in the heart of the mission. Cultural humility, when authentic, is a system people's way of saying, "We have done great harm, and we shall never go that way again." Ultimately, it is a faith in those devalued peoples. That they are true and full human beings, with every sacred right and power to heal themselves. That the system is not to be the great authority, but the willing student and helper. And that the people must be, now and forever, regarded sacredly.

I see a hopeful resolution here. A way that does not rely on naively seeking to *train and inform* people into treating others better while neglecting the hateful, putrid spirit in our common culture that violates vulnerable people. Instead of finding impotent training language to make people feel comfortable with their prejudice and cultural supremacy, we can create workplaces that foster a sense of wellness, security, and safety. This in turn allows people to feel more comfortable reckoning with their social illnesses. Cultivating a spirit and practice of mutual care, people can develop a real motive for reckoning with the seeds of their sickness. Mutual care and workforce wellness don't just improve morale and retention. These dynamics actually buttress personal healing and growth in workers and leaders. Transformation that can cause system people to relate to communities with more humanity. Humane servitude has a chance to fertilize healing, in both communities and workforces. This is the only way that numbers, statistics, and precious quantifiable outcomes can be reversed into the direction of wellness, and stay there.

Mutual care inspires self-care and socialization toward wholeness. This in turn germinates healing from inner prejudice and supremacy, two of the most drastic vicarious traumas. As systems and agencies become mutually caring in spirit, then recruitment, hiring, and professional development all take on a cultural maintenance role. We become more mindful of the kinds of people we recruit and hire. Technical skill is no longer sufficient qualification alone. Character becomes paramount. We make it clear to job applicants that our tribe is not one you should join if you are socially ill and do not care deeply about working in harmony with colleagues and community. We screen out those who would pollute our climate of mutual care, and encourage them to self-select into another line of work.

We promote to the community that our work tribe and its people are of a new era. One in which the work is about rehumanizing the dehumanized, within us and among us. We acknowledge our personal and collective social illness, empowering ourselves to treat it. We learn the language that calls our poison what it is, so that we can eradicate it. We no longer speak around the truth, or find programmatic hideaways from the critical work we cannot avoid. No more codependent, avoidant language or approaches. No more pretending or fearful shuffling. We are healers. We treat what is wounded and hurting. We muster reason, will, and courage, and we begin.

LOVE THE ONES YOU SERVE

Make sure you Love the ones you serve. If you do not, your servitude becomes a mutually painful burden. If you are not caring for yourself, the poisonous seeds planted in you since childhood, the false ideas about other people and cultures, can germinate and sprout. Workplace stress, negativity, and trauma can be like an acid rain that feeds these tainted sprouts. Eventually you become a forest of bitterness and resentment toward the people whose lives you are meant to bless. You suffer greatly. Your compassion stream slows to a meager trickle, then stops running altogether. You see no beauty in your work, creating an eclipse of beauty in your life. If this is you, friend, claiming this truth is a gift, to all. It is the beginning of your reclamation of Love.

This work is for Lovers. It is too challenging not to be. If you are out on a long hike in nature, you bring water with you, and you drink it. If you are out on a long journey of serving human lives, you bring Love with you, and you drink from it. It gets you through the day, your nectar of sustenance. Love and its breath of compassion cause you to be great at finding ways to help someone. Your greatness then turns inward, and you become devoted to caring for yourself. Activated Love in your heart is a tranquilizer: It dims your stress and fear. It is a motivator, inspiring you into passion that makes your workday a blessing and a celebration. So if your Love faucet is not working, repair it. Spend time feeling Love and Love will come. When you start gushing again, now you are a proper healer, renewed and worthy of your sacred work.

We have a public duty to cultivate a Loving spirit for those we serve, and those with whom we serve. If we do not, we become a harmful presence in their lives, and defeat our ideal of servitude. Further, we generate our own suffering. Loving spirit is our first duty, before meeting quotas and closing cases. Before compliance and protocol. Without Loving spirit, our bureaucratic endeavors are poisoned and distorted. They betray the healing potential for which our systems exist in the first place. If we are to be consumed with quotas, let us be consumed with a *Love quota*. Ask daily: *Have I Loved all that I can? Have we?* And if we are wed to compliance, let us be compliant to Love. Love is not so difficult to measure. It is the shimmering evidence of how much we care, tangible in the way we make people feel.

DUNGEONS AND DRAGONS

If you make people do their work in dungeons, many of them will turn into dragons. This is one of the most blatantly self-destructive traditions of helping systems: Drab walls and floors. Stale air and harsh lighting. And the sound of... human anxiety. This is the state of many buildings and office where lives are served. As though we aim to punish the people who need services for failing to be spectacular and thriving. But it is our workers and leaders who are punished the most by depressing environments. They are the ones who spend the most time in these spaces. Why are we so afraid of soothing, cheerful colors on our walls? Of bright windows flooding our offices with the natural stress suppressor known as sunlight? Many of the sessions I have conducted with agencies have been in rooms as dark as dusk. I arrive and people are sitting in the dark like vampires. No one has thought to open the blinds and let in some sunlight. This is clearly a habitual state of existence. Are we depressed? Our behavior and habits, not to mention our buildings and interiors, suggest so. Let us dream of one day doing this work in atmospheres that feel joyful and hopeful, for the sake of workers, leaders, and the hurting ones who visit our spaces. Murals on the walls portraying promising stories. Artwork that brings smiles and laughter. Scents that make us feel good. Fresh air. Big windows. There is a psychology to interior design. We become our environment. Time for an art project.

MUSIC IS MEDICINE

Why is it that in the most stressful jobs, society has decided that this is where it will banish music from the environment? I often play music in my sessions with staff. At the first notes, people stop chatting and look in my direction with expressions on their faces like children being introduced to ice cream. Something feels good to them, stirs their soul. And yet, the presence of music at work is so foreign that some of them verge on being traumatized with shock. Many of these same people blast music in their cars on the way home, and dance like dervishes at the gym or club. But at work, we are so zombied-out that we react to music like fairytale witches to water. How about we go from zombie to Zen? Countless research shows how music affects the brain and body. Music calms and energizes us. Lifts our mood. Improves memory and performance. Facilitates social bonding. You would think that music would be a central feature of social and human service hallways and offices. But no, *we must be grim. We have serious work to do.* Seriously? What is this, the town prohibition from *Footloose?* Music therapy is happening everywhere these days. Except in the public service spaces that so dearly need it. If we can't change the windows, walls, or carpet, let's at least allow ourselves some tunes.

FEAR MONGERS

Fear mongers dwell among you. What to do with them? Well, what do you do when someone's cigarette smoke clouds your face? You close your eyes, stop inhaling, and whisk the smoke away. Do the same when someone blows fear clouds into the workplace, or into a conversation. Close your social intake valves, actively reject and whisk away the fear. Speak optimism and purpose into the air. Do it for you. Do it for your tribe. Take charge of the atmosphere. Some people are *need workers*, and focus on serving the real needs of others. Some people are *fear workers*, and have a taste for spreading fear. Send your fear workers out on frequent errands, like to the taco truck to pick up snacks and drinks. Just kidding. Don't banish people. It's not nice. But do take measures not to let your fear workers rule the day. Need workers are among you, and they are on a mission. You know which campaign to join. You might even choose to lead the cause.

POOH AND EEYORE

Winnie the Pooh is quite a joyful fellow. He tends to see the brighter side of life and exude a childlike quality of wonder. So whenever Pooh rolls up on his boy Eeyore, he is naturally excited to see his close friend. With exuberance in his voice and a marvelous smiley, Pooh greets Eeyore: "Hello, Friend! How are you doing today?"

Regardless of the weather or circumstance, Eeyore responds with a sullen, self-pitying, depressed, pessimistic moan: "Oooooh.... Okay, I guess. Could be better..." Eeyore, you see, is the sweetest of souls, but he is also chronically embedded in the *woe-is-me* of gloom and doom. We should give him a break. He does have a tail nailed to his butt after all. Chronic pain like this can bring a person down, right? But it bruises Pooh's Poohish heart to see his dear buddy in such sorrow. Try as he might, Pooh can never quite lift Eeyore out of his valley of despair.

You have people like this in your life, yes? In your work? Take a moment and consider your Eeyores. Maybe you are an Eeyore, bless your heart. It's a good thing you found this book. Yes, consider the Eeyores in your life. Let's say it's evening and you're kicking back, relaxing. You want to pick up the phone and call a friend or family member, just to say hi. Just as you are ready to call, you realize: *I'm about to call an Eeyore.* Your whole body sags at the thought. You know that as soon as the conversation starts, the Eeyore doom and gloom will come pouring through the phone line and energy will drain out of you faster than a popped balloon. By the end of the call, you will be so exhausted you'll have no choice but to go to bed. And you might end up so down and low that you eat half a carton of ice cream. Which isn't an unpleasant thought, but still. This whole scenario runs through your mind in a flash. You put down the phone and go back to watching reality television. *This,* my friend, is the resounding impact of Eeyore energy.

Every workplace has its Poohs and Eeyores. The Poohs generally were born as Poohs. They can't help but to spread sunshine and see the brighter side of life. The Eeyores, however, may have been born with a tail nailed to their butt, or... this work may have nailed it there. This work, and more likely the culture of the work, may have sunk a long nail deep into their booty. Not able to recognize this trauma, and not knowing how to remove the nail, they have become saturated with and encased within lament, complaint, negativity, moans, and wailing. You Love and care for them, but their energy drains you and the whole group. You've tried many times to help them remove the nail that is causing so much pain. But the peculiar thing about Eeyores is they resist relief, happiness, and hope. This is part of being in the Eeyore condition. You can offer them every workplace change imaginable to meet their needs and grievances, and they will only wail louder. You see, being an Eeyore is a self-fulfilling prophecy. The wonderful thing, though, is that so is being a Pooh.

Celebrate your Poohs. Celebrate, profile, encourage, and support your Poohs. They may be experiencing resistance or even resentment from their Eeyore friends. In many ways, group morale and spirit are a tug of war between Poohship and Eeyoreship. Whichever clique puts more energy into tugging on the rope can determine the day. Or the year. Place Poohs in leadership positions, informal and formal. Ensure they are entrenched as your tribe's story gatherers and tellers. Involve them in recruitment, hiring, initiation, orientation, and ongoing development. Use your Poohs. Don't let their light go undirected.

If you are an Eeyore, my friend, don't beat yourself up about it. See this as a sign that you could use some Love and care, most of all from yourself. Choose to go on various retreats, away from the work or just away from your mental habits. Commit yourself to gently retraining your thoughts into a state of gratitude and appreciation, which generates calming hormones that diminish stress.

We can't have professional Eeyores serving community Eeyores in crisis. *No bueno.* Agency cultures need to have vision, process, and priority in place to continuously rehabilitate Eeyore spirit. Not Eeyore *people*, but Eeyore spirit pervasive in our atmosphere. Gently support those with Eeyore spirit to retrain themselves. Sometimes, seasoned staff forget who they are. They use their position, their badge and title, their tenure and unreleased tantrums as brute force for a kind of hazing of new workers. Condescending tones and horror stories pour from them like silt water after a storm. And, bless them, for they have been through heavy storms. Help these helpers who have forgotten their inner helper. Find ways to stir their memory and bring them home.

MUTE THE DOUBTERS

Plenty of your colleagues are likely to say to you that transforming your organization is impossible, unrealistic, fool's gold. Kindly put these people on mute. Banish their opinion to the distant place in your mind. These people may mean well, but their words reflect fear, pessimism, and most of all, presumption. They cannot know what is impossible. They have not done absolute, conclusive research on every agency and system that has attempted to rehabilitate itself. The fact and truth is that it has been done. Therefore it can be done. Difficulty should not be equated with impossibility. If it were, no progress would ever be made in this world. Yet it is. Every moment and day. So put doubt and resistance in their proper place, far away from your courageous spirit of change.

VIRAL DYSFUNCTION

There is a viral nature to dysfunction in people and groups. A generational persistence to dysfunction caused by dysfunction's ability to mutate within its host, to survive change and develop resistance to wellness. For this reason, your personal change campaign must be *intentional, convicted, and supercharged*. The same is true for any system rehabilitation. We cannot afford to be casual, passive, or half-hearted in our efforts, and then end up wondering why nothing has really changed. And actual sickness is within us. Our immune system can resolve this, but it needs to be fortified.

POUR TEA

In a region of the world including Tibet, Nepal, Afghanistan, and Pakistan, a cultural idea exists that can be expressed in the English language as *pouring tea*. When I was living and studying in Nepal during college, I had the opportunity to conduct independent research. I chose to learn about healing and wellness from the area's Tibetan Holistic Doctors. These doctors are the equivalent of a social worker, medical doctor, nurse, therapist, guide, mentor, coach, parent, and friend, all in one. Truly holistic practitioners of healing and wellness. Social and human service professionals. Helpers, like you.

The Tibetan doctors explained to me the idea of *pouring tea* this way: "Instead of valuing process over relationships, we Tibetans are socialized since birth within our culture to view relationships as the means by which processes may be best completed. When someone comes to us in need, we do not rush into an anxious processing of information. Rather, we pour a cup of tea. The tea itself, the pouring, the offering and accepting, the taking time to drink together—all of this is a statement and act of relationship building. With the first cup of tea, we take the relationship from stranger status to familiarity.

"This is not enough. Even if time appears to be limited for us, or for the one in need, we understand that by rushing and devaluing the relationship, we will ultimately cost ourselves time. So, we pour a second cup of tea. This shared experience takes the relationship from familiarity to friendship. We then pour a third cup of tea, which takes us from friendship to being family. It is mutually understood that once we consider each other family, in the sense of meaningful interdependence, we will care for each other and think and act on behalf of each other's wellbeing."

I sat, humbled and awed, as I listened to one after another Tibetan doctor share this same story with me. I began to reflect on our own society's perpetual anxiety, stress, rushing, and neglect of relationship. This way of being doesn't seem to benefit our wellness, does it? I learned from my Tibetan brothers and sisters that it is not actual tea that makes the difference. In our culture here, tea can be an example or symbol of *caring enough to share and connect* in order to empower both the practitioner and the one in need to work together toward wellness, stability, and prosperity.

We operate under a mistaken belief that if only we focus more frantically on the process, then somehow we will get the process done more quickly and effectively. This is like believing if we sprint across our lawn with a manual lawnmower, we will get the job done quicker and more effectively. Just the opposite, as we well know. Rushing like this, neglecting the details and intimacy of the moment, we only end up having to go back over our lawn to complete the job sufficiently. This happens continuously in service to human lives. The true job, building relationship to support service delivery and human healing, is neglected rampantly. We may get the paperwork done, but the relational work hasn't been done. As a result, the people in need remain underserved, disempowered to change their reality, and vulnerable. They remain in our system as a result. This leaves someone with yet more paperwork and processing to do. A worker may feel that he has swiftly moved through the case, freeing himself up for the next one. In reality, he has only backed up the entire system. A backup that in many ways comes back to haunt and impact him.

Pouring tea can happen in an instant: In the way we greet others, in our tone of voice, in the way we ask about their life. Taking a deep breath together is a cup of tea. Sharing your human reality is a cup of tea. Offering a cup of water, or a piece of fruit. Laughing together. Listening. The excuse that we don't have time to pour three cups of tea is just that: an excuse. It is not reality, just cultural conditioning. And remember, the tea you pour is not only serving others, it is serving you. You are blessing your capacity to be well, attentive, sensitive, and helpful in the moment, and in the process. Take a deep breath, friend. Pour some tea.

HORIZONTAL RELATIONSHIPS

One of the other priceless lessons the Tibetan doctors shared with me is the way their culture conditions them to think about those they serve. Consistently, each of these social servants said to me, "Jivan Dai (their Nepali name for me), we are taught that when someone in need comes to us, our first thought is not, *Oh no, here is yet another case to burden my load.* To think in this way instantly creates a vertical relationship in which I place myself as helper at the top of the ladder and the one in need at the bottom of the ladder. In this relationship arrangement, I have set myself up to be less effective in my work. Looking down from the top of the ladder, I cannot see the whole person, only one dimension, usually a misleading one. And the person in need, looking up from the bottom of the ladder, can only see my bottom, literally. This is not the most flattering view, and again, withholds my whole, true self from the person who needs to be in relationship with me."

These Tibetan practitioners went on to say, "Our culture teaches us that when a person in need comes to us, our first thought should be, *Hey! Life thinks so much of me, it has granted me with a new teacher!* Reacting like this, I set myself up for success in my work. My attitude is gratitude and not grievance, resentment, or negativity. I have instantly positioned myself and the person in need into a horizontal relationship. "

When you are a helper or a healer, horizontal relationships are your best friend. They allow for healing elements to flow in both directions. Both people receive the nutrition and irrigation of relationship: trust, openness, sharing, relaxed creativity and problem solving, listening, kind speech, positivity, hopefulness, and affection. Why banish all of this wonderful resource from your act of service by condescending to the person as just another burden in your work and life? Humility is a quality of grace. A shedding of all that gets in the way of us honoring each other.

The one who comes to us is a gift. This person brings a lesson about what it means to be human under the particular conditions and journey of her or his life. So many people in need. So many gifts. Why refuse the offering and choose to suffer in the work? Give both people in the equation the best opportunity to see each other. No deception, professional masks and postures, or illusions. Just the simple person you are and the simple person they are, meeting in a place of honor and caring to share a story, giving that story oxygen to transform and grow. Power, authority, and control are seductive drugs for us when we are fearful, insecure, tired, and stressed. But they do nothing for true servitude. And they sicken all parties. *Humility.* The act of choosing a horizontal relationship. Here is where the good things grow.

TEACHER IS THE STUDENT

Every person who is charged with leading, supervising, managing, or mentoring you, practice seeing them as your students. They may have a formal duty to guide you, but the spirit and dynamic of mutual care says that your relationship is evidence that you have something for them as well. Assume that they have lessons to learn from you, even if they don't realize it. Engage with them as an active student by not putting on them the burden of your passiveness and dependence. Be interdependent with them. Share freely. This will encourage you to receive freely. This kind of reciprocity creates a draft. A breezeway. Seeds of growth are blown in both directions, land and take hold in both of you. Your way of being a student matters. It affects and shapes your teacher. Empower them in their role by caring as much about what they are learning as what they are teaching.

STUDENT IS THE TEACHER

Practice seeing as your teacher every person you are charged with serving, leading, supervising, managing, or mentoring. Doing so will humble and open you to receive so much more from the relationship. Your presence and persona will feel better to that person. He or she will feel safer with you, open more, share more, and will become an empowered learner. Your teaching will grow more fertile, effective. You won't feel such a sense of burden. Rather, you will sense fortune visiting you.

HUMILITY

We are not some superior species, serving pitiable souls from afar. We *are* the community. We grow up in them, arise from them. We should see them as our origin, even if we come from a different geography or culture. People have more respect and honor for what they consider their origin. Understanding that we professionals are the artifacts and outcomes of the communities we serve enlightens us to the intimate interdependency we share. This truth is humbling, which leaves us right where we need to be in relation to the community: on their level, not above. Their afflictions suggest the seeds in us of our own. Their healing and prosperity should indicate to us our personal promise. We lose so much when we relate to communities as people beneath and foreign to us. Regardless of cultural persona, those we serve are the source of our beginning, and the delta of our destination. We are all going someplace together. Our hope lies in caring enough about the sacred journey.

APPRECIATION

Annual staff appreciation events are common. But if the other 364 days of the year aren't filled with appreciation, then that one event can feel to staff like a token effort. A dishonest attempt to appease. If this happens, your staff appreciation event may have made matters worse, creating a contrast, highlighting the 364 days people don't feel appreciated. We can't starve people, then hand them a crumb and expect them to feel well fed. You can't fake the funk with appreciation. It can't be half-stepped. It must be full bodied and flush. Management should ensure that in the midst of the arduous task of leadership, it hasn't taken staff for granted. Staff should do the same. And staff can also give themselves permission to freely appreciate each other and management. This is helpful for management, who too often confuse leadership with the need to outwardly pose in self-denial.

Appreciation is an organic thing. We need to allow it to emerge and spread organically. It belongs inside of habit, not on schedule calendars. It cannot breathe there. It breathes inside of intention and heartfelt repetition. We must practice expressing appreciation for ourselves, each other, and the larger tribe or agency, until practice becomes habit. Get in the habit of sharing appreciation notes with each other, regardless of title. Remember the notes we shared in school growing up? Some of you were passionate and creative note makers. Your notes were works of art, complete with multiple-choice questions (friends, best friends, more than friends?), graphic art, and flourishes of color. What happened? Why did we stop passing notes to each other? Do it at work. You will make someone's day. And when you receive one, your day will be made.

Before rushing forward too far into our grand celebration and appreciation plans, it helps to ask people how they prefer to be recognized or celebrated. Some want the whole fiesta—piñata and all. Others are averse to so much attention. For them, quiet recognition is sufficient and soothing. It helps to ask.

Acknowledging others and expressing appreciation places the initiators in teaching roles, where they get to share what something has meant to them. This can bolster morale, esteem, confidence, and sense of belonging.

If you are assigned credit for something good in your workplace, make sure the credit trickles down and migrates up. All happenings at work are social. We see this if we care to look closely. When credit is assigned, most of the people involved, even in the most granular, indirect ways, are left out of the recognition. Credit hoarders create credit debt in their tribe. Credit sharers bless the tribe with a spirit of communion.

Every staff or management meeting can be seen as a great chance for peer-to-peer recognition and appreciation. Is there a better time than when we are with each other? We need only put it on the agenda. As appreciation is expressed throughout the year, pressure is taken off an annual event, an event that now feels sincerer to all involved. Staff are going through heartbreak with the people they serve. In a deeply human way, these professionals deserve and need daily appreciation. There is no such thing as over-appreciation, though many leaders act as though they are afraid of this happening. People can be held to high standards and a strong work ethic and still be lavished in praise. The two flows are not mutually exclusive. Rather, they feed each other. Those who don't believe this are likely not to have tried expressing unbridled appreciation, nor to have received it. Go ahead, grow intoxicated together on appreciation. No hangovers have ever been reported.

AFFIRMATION

When a child cries, its deepest message to us is not, "Stop my crying." It is instead, "Notice me." For to be seen, truly seen, is the beginning of our human sense of security, and of our capacity to heal the personal pain that brings our tears. The human soul is crying. Here's to all of you who care to stop and truly see. Now, it is time for you to be seen. By the ones with whom you work. Distilling workplace laments, grievances, complaints, and unspoken dissatisfactions and hurts, we can see that workers and leaders both want something very simple and exact: *affirmation.*

And yet, time and again, leaders will not affirm their staff. And staff will not affirm their leaders. This is a shame, for all work communications can be pregnant with affirmation, if we so choose. Affirmation is essential to human wellness. If we cannot get it from the world, we better be able to at least get it from ourselves, and even then, self-affirmation is not entirely sufficient. We are each living a social experience. A phenomenon of relationship. Affirmation grounds us, locates us, clarifies us, emboldens us. It is compass, map, terrain, and gauge. In the African cultural sense affirmation says, "I see you," and in being seen, we experience our most secure regard since the womb.

CELEBRATION

In our mainstream culture, the concept of celebrating is often associated with superficial, surface-level, and trivial activity. Throughout human history, though, celebration has been understood as a primary, affirming method of maintaining the strength, wellness, bonds, traditions, and values of a cultural community. We should always look for reasons to celebrate in our work. Small, granular reasons are just as meaningful as obvious, grandiose reasons. Even celebrating our togetherness and achievements in the work adds value and is worthy. There is an intimacy to celebration that brings us into each other's atmosphere of emotion and spirit. Each time we celebrate is like coming up from beneath the water for air. We inhale something that sustains us when we go back under.

I am not necessarily suggesting that we take extra time to celebrate, but that we at least learn to celebrate within the natural flow of our work processes. It is possible for us to build celebration even into the reporting out we do at meetings. We are enriching our standard moments, not necessarily taking more time. Celebration lubricates labor, saving time in the end.

Celebration is most effective when it is regular and consistent, not rare or periodic. Consistency feels more sincere. Celebrate loudly. Not in terms of volume, but by letting the larger agency and community know what you are celebrating. This can model for them the value of celebration. Celebrate quietly. Not in terms of volume, but by permitting yourselves to celebrate in small ways, and by celebrating even the smallest of things. Clearly identify the reasons for your celebration, no matter how foolish they seem. Self-proclaimed fools make for the freest celebrators. Celebrate verbally in the way you communicate with each other. Celebrate in writing, even as a part of your broader communication with each other.

Celebrate redundantly. Too much celebration is generally better than too little when it comes to morale, teambuilding, stress release, and many other benefits. Widely promote the story of your celebration itself, not just the reason behind it. It feeds and inspires others. Celebrate organically and creatively. It doesn't always have to be so bureaucratic and forced. Celebrate both spontaneously and through thoughtful planning. Celebrate inclusively. Use it as an opportunity to invite those from outside your group. Continuously remind each other of the value of celebration until it becomes cultural habit. Use celebration as a reminder of your change-initiative values and goals. Recruit peer celebrators, the party animals among you. Condition everyone to be empowered to kick-off a celebration.

There will always be people among you looking for reasons not to celebrate. They will hunt barriers like treasure hunters seek gems in the sand. These people will try to make you feel guilty about celebrating. They will say, "We don't have the time, money, or energy to be celebrating. And besides, we have too much work to do." Maybe these people didn't get enough ice cream as children. Or maybe they ate too much of it. Remind yourself and your group that if you don't celebrate, you will lose far more time, money, and energy, because you will lose people from the work. Beaten down and depleted, they will leave the job. Beyond that, true celebration doesn't take time, money, or energy. It is an act in the heart, manifest in the social environment that lubricates and gives soul to our work. Guilt about feeling good is an artifact of socialization in an unwell culture. Talk yourself out of that guilt. Give yourself permission to be joyful. This is how you respect and honor your servitude.

ALWAYS BE CELEBRATING (ABC)

Healthy social and human service organizations must be passionate, devoted, and continuous in celebrating their work. Stress, anxiety, trauma, and crisis are ever present. Celebration is a hydraulic system purging all of this away. Stories, memories, shared laughter and tears, values, wisdom, lessons, grieving, honoring, dreaming, conspiring beautifully... this is how celebration does what it does.

A healthy cardiovascular system is openly flowing, delivering nutrition, healing, and growth factors directly to where the body needs them. For a social service system, celebration is that flow. Celebration is not trivial. It is a primary tonic for wellness. And remember, whatever you are not celebrating, you are practicing *not celebrating*. If you aren't celebrating your work, then you are becoming better at not celebrating your work. There is no neutral. We celebrate the good things in our work, or we become better at not celebrating them. Into that void, negativity and unhappiness are more than willing to step. So practice the joy and appreciation that come with celebration.

Celebrate everything. Even the most embarrassing, foolish things. Someone's new braces. Personal milestones. The person who tells unfunny jokes and falls out laughing. The weather. A new office plant. Go wild with celebration. Don't be ashamed of celebrating, or the ways you or your group celebrates. Self-consciousness kills many celebrations before they even take their first breath. Don't let social anxieties get in the way of your full-time party. Your work will thank you.

HOUSE PARTY

When I was a professor, I looked for every reason for each class session to be a celebration: A student's birthday. Someone's dog's birthday. A personal achievement. Or even just the fact that we were fortunate enough to be gathered together on a particular day. Word quickly spread that the classes I taught, regardless of subject, were where the party was happening. We didn't stop there. I cooked meals and brought them. Soon, students joined in and brought food, artwork, music. I stood atop my desk and recited spoken word, regularly. Sometimes to highlight a subject matter, other times just because it felt good to me, and hopefully, to the students. I invited them to share their talents and passions with their classmates. Students sang, danced, played instruments, shared poetry and stories. They formed groups, rehearsed, and performed dramatic skits. Some students had never recited anything before an audience before, yet would find the courage to stand before their classmates and bless us with their inspiration. Whatever a student's thing was, that's what we invited to the party.

Registration soared. Attendance bloomed. Disengaged students moved from the back seats to the front rows. I did not think of my work as *psychology*. I thought of it as creating a space in which people were open to growing into psychology, and their own life. Our classroom was not for soulless dictation of information in a one-way current from teacher to student. Our classroom was a greenhouse. A fertile, inviting space where students felt free to discover themselves. Through this self-discovery they were not passive recipients of classroom information. They were active learners and teachers, generating the curriculum from their own lives and cultural validity. It was for me one of the most meaningful times of my life.

Our workplaces don't have to be dreary. Our work does not have to be monotonous. Whatever our job title or agency sector, we can define our work as creating a space that feels safe, that invites people to bring and share their passions and culture. This is how we empower ourselves to serve the massive variety of human cultures in our communities. By enriching our cultural workplace lives, daily, not during some marginalized month of observation. We can define our work as the daily act of awakening the Loving, creative spirit in our nature of greatness. If we do this right, our workplace will develop a reputation: We will be where the house party is at, and so many good souls will want to come and stay.

FEAST DAY

In the American Indian communities of northern New Mexico exists a tradition called Feast Day, a sacred occasion for ceremonial dance, communal feasting, and celebration of community. In one Feast Day tradition, the entire Pueblo Indian community moves as a sea of souls from home to home. The family of each home gathers on their rooftop. All the generations are present. In an act of Grace, oneness, and reciprocity, each family member joyfully throws their stores of food and drink and other useful items down to the crowd below. The crowd roars and bustles to receive the offering. The host family knows something fundamental to their culture: They are not giving their provisions away. Rather, they are sharing them with the community that will in turn pour even more back into their lives.

Then, wave after wave of the crowd is invited into the family's home. They wait along the walls until the group before them has finished eating. Then they take their place. The host family keeps the food and drink coming. The long table is always full. And even as the guests fill their bellies, they are urged continuously by the hosts: "*Eat plenty. Eat plenty...*"

Workers, teams, and organizations in mainstream culture have been conditioned to exist in a manner that is a polar opposite to Feast Day: Territoriality. Distrust. Hoarding of resources, relationships, and success stories. Perceiving others outside the person or group as adversaries. This spirit operates in many human serving organizations. It is sad that we are so stuck in a self-destructive, self-suffocating mentality. This belief system, and culture, drains groups of their vitality and health. All because we fail to believe in a central foundation of communal life: When we share with each other, we receive back much more than what we have shared. This is difficult for our individualistic, fragmented, competitive culture to believe in. So we practice existing in claustrophobic silos.

Wouldn't it be revolutionary for workers and groups to practice intentional sharing, instead of reacting to stress and crisis by shrinking and closing? It is possible to make each day at work a feast day. An open invitation to the human community of coworkers to surround our personal or team home, so that we may pour our provisions out to the masses. We can redefine what we feel is ours to keep and ours to give. We can gather our life and skill resources and be gracious in sharing our Love, kindness, patience, and compassion. Then we can invite the whole pueblo (group) inside the home of our Goodness, where we joyfully serve every single soul, wave after wave, with our meals of hospitality: decency, generosity, and communal bonding. And with each trip to fill our table with bounty for our worldly guests, we too can urge these hungry souls with our Loving appeal: "Please, e*at plenty.*"

Let's make every day a feast day. A continuous habit of celebration and communion. A backdrop to our fatiguing processes and procedures. So that this work will be a more sacred place and phenomenon. *Eat Plenty* can be a personal, group, and tribe mantra. A prompt for how we engage with our self-care, with our coworkers and leadership, and with the humans who make up our caseload. *Eat Plenty* can be a private reminder to breathe, and to stay calm, open, and centered in a stressful moment or period. *Eat Plenty* can be a leadership philosophy, an ongoing recruitment and retention theme, and a teambuilding call to action.

EMPOWER YOUR LEADERS

Just as staff need to be empowered by formal leadership to be at their best, in a mutually caring, healthy organization, leadership needs to be empowered by staff. Leadership needs Love, too. They are human and have human fears, insecurities, and challenges. Leaders are often starved of honest, caring feedback. They suffer from a drought of meaningful insight. Workers assume that leaders know everything workers are feeling, saying, dealing with, so they keep that information to themselves. Or, workers don't want to impose on what they imagine are overflowing leadership cups. Feed your leaders by sharing with them in caring ways.

We tend to assume that people know how to lead, and therefore if they are doing it poorly it is because they don't care. But so many people have never really had good leadership examples. Not growing up, or in their life or work. Some are scared to death of leading, avoid leadership like the plague, believing it easier to follow. They work harder at remaining mediocre than it would take to excel. Resist growth so they can maintain their security blanket of a life in the ruts. But in the end, nothing is harder or more burdensome than a lifetime of not becoming what you were born to be. It is compassionate and wise of us to assume that people could use our leadership support and guidance, our feedback and insight, even if we are staff and those people are our formal leaders. This is how mutual care wonderfully thinks: *That person, with whom I work and am interdependent, could use my help.*

In a mutually caring system or group, staff contribute to supervisor evaluations, supervisors to manager evaluations, and on up the ladder. In a hostile environment, this idea may be rejected passionately. But on the way toward healing, it is a tribal practice that creates abundant growth.

Learn to be a culture that feeds its leaders. You will have healthier, more responsive leaders. Pass them appreciation notes. Give them real and symbolic pats on the back. Encourage them for the job they are doing. Don't choose to make them your adversary. Choose to make them your exemplary. Don't idealize or idolize them. This is destructive to all involved. Let them be human even if they carry themselves as though they feel they need to be superhuman. That mantle is exhausting and cannot be sustained. So encourage them, caringly, to let down their guard, take off their mask, and join the crazy human party going on. Because it is certainly going on, isn't it?

Empower your leadership by not bringing them all of the things that you can truly handle on your own. Don't put your stuff on their plate. Clean your own plate. Believe in yourself. This helps leaders immensely. Be aware of how you bring things to your leaders. It is careless and harmful to continuously bring them your panic, stress, fear, and trauma in addition to actual work items. When you do this, you overwhelm them from their true leadership duty and are harming yourself. If you feel some of your leaders don't know how to lead, you can spend the rest of your days together beating them down, or building them up. If you have leadership skills of your own, find ways to offer them to your challenged leaders. Each of us has special needs, bless our hearts. And we need people's compassion and support to overcome them.

TRAUMA TRAVELS UPWARD

Think of how the toxic element mercury concentrates in the ocean's food chain: microorganisms and plankton feed on the mercury, which then concentrates in their body. Small fish feed on the plankton. Large fish feed on the small fish. On and on up the ladder, the mercury gets passed, becoming more concentrated along the way. Trauma and stress from a community enters the hierarchy of an agency in the same way, traveling up the ladder from staff to leadership. The more responsibility a leader has, the more vulnerable that person is to internalizing concentrated levels of trauma and stress. The reason for this is *exponential responsibility.* The more people for whom you are responsible, the more vulnerable you become. For this reason, leaders need to be very conscious and aware of how vicarious trauma and stress might be affecting their wellness. And most importantly, staff need to realize their mutual care responsibility to leadership: Commit to bringing leadership positive energy and expression, regardless of the crisis or conflict.

In a relay race, team members must practice handing off the baton to each other without losing momentum, and without dropping the baton. In an organization this translates into staff acting from a place of capability and giftedness and not fear, insecurity, or incapability. When the latter happens, the momentum of serving lives gets lost. When staff drop the baton of fulfilling their role, beyond their job title, in the full spirit of devoted servitude, the impact ripples upward through leadership. This creates a sometimes crippling burden on leaders who have to run their segment of the race as well as that of staff. Taking the baton involves staff committing to critical thinking, problem solving, and creative resolution. These are life and professional skills (muscles to be exercised) necessary for anyone who wishes to grow, blossom, and fulfill her or his potential. Staff possess intelligence, brilliance, creativity, and resourcefulness. When these gifts are tapped and flowing regularly, leaders are freed and empowered to fulfill their own roles.

MIDDLE MANAGEMENT NEEDS LOVE, TOO

Supervisors and managers are often referred to as middle management. And what are they in the middle of? Not titles and positions, but real relationships involving those they lead and those by whom they are led. This is unique territory. Responsibility to lead staff brings a pressure that can be intensified by the gravitational weight of being led in turn by executive management.

A sandwiching of souls, if you will. A certain freedom to lead that is at the same time limited by not having ultimate authority. Middle managers, then, have two collective bodies to satisfy, at seemingly opposite ends of a continuum of concern. They are, in fact, liaisons for both parties.

Have you ever tried to build up your confidence while the conditions of your life seem to conspire to tear it down? Middle managers strive to believe in themselves as leaders, but as they have their own authorities *above* them, this can have a dampening effect on self-confidence. On sense of efficacy. This can create a vacillation in identity and self-security. A confusion of loyalties. And a self-perception of conflict. For these reasons and more, middle managers need mucho Love. And they need each other greatly. But system life can foster isolation, individuation, and territoriality. What is the tonic for these maladies?

Tribal time. Middle managers meet regularly to report out to each other on numbers, policy, and other bureaucracy concerns. They come together and leave once more, not having taken advantage of their role kinship. But what were their deeper needs heading into these meetings? Support. Affirmation. Learning and mentoring. Evidence that with their plate of challenges, they are not alone.

Instead of only reporting out to each other, these leaders need to be feeding each other, feeding from each other. They are hungry for nutritional stories: what is working for this person, what that team has discovered, what this unit is attempting. They need an agenda of laughter, cleansing tears, remembrance, broadening of perspective, lightening of heart.

Tribal time together grants these liaison leaders space and time for building each other up, and fortifying their collective leadership. An agency can only benefit from a socially strong, empowered middle management. *Support groups* are what I'm getting at. Teambuilding tends to focus on a supervisor and her or his staff. Just as much need exists between middle managers in the cohering and strengthening of their own team. If you are one of these liaison leaders, strive with your leader-peers to build retreat opportunities into your work. Not necessarily weekends or full days. Even 15 minutes of kinship kindling with other middle managers can do wonders. In-person is great, but when this isn't possible, it shouldn't be an excuse not to connect. Tribal time happens when people want it to happen. Life can be funny like that.

HUMANIZE YOUR FORMAL LEADERS

Staff can act strangely toward you as a formal leader, yes? Maybe you were in a regular staff role, then were promoted, and suddenly your colleagues related to you differently? Do they freak out when you call or appear on the scene? Much of this is because of how we all experienced authority as children. It was frightening, mystifying, and often oppressive. To humanize yourself to staff, you will all need to work together to demystify your role and the person within the role.

Be real. Show your humanness. Share the story of your journey. Acknowledge your fears and insecurities about your leadership role, and the need for appreciation. Don't be afraid to laugh and cry freely with your staff. Ask for support. Invite staff to formally and informally mentor you in your staff relations. Regularly share your leadership considerations, pressures, processes, and decision-making challenges. Essentially, open your door. Both your office door, and the door of authority that can unnecessarily feel like a brick wall between you and the staff you care so much to supportively lead. Your staff aren't praying that secretly you are a robot. They are praying that you are a caring, feeling human being. Show them.

VULNERABILITY

Power and control do not build trust. Vulnerability does. Whether or not you are a formal leader, being vulnerable helps your colleagues and service recipients feel safe with you, relate to you, and experience compassion for your unique realities and challenges. The unhealthier the workplace, the more likely we are to find a culture that says *vulnerability is bad*. Since you are now entirely convinced (smile) that vulnerability can be a relationship and service instrument, here is a quick sketch for fostering vulnerability between you and others: Share your stories. Acknowledge your needs, fears, hopes. Admit your mistakes and growth journeys. Openly ask for support and collaboration. Bow down in humility and look up in admiration. This does wonders for social bonds. Express your admiration. Make it known. Reveal your heart. Listen, listen, listen... And when you ask yourself what you do for a living, say this mantra inside your soul: *I am a vulnerability worker.*

EMPOWER YOUR STAFF

Staff, regardless of skills and experience, can often exist in a state of disempowerment, simply as a result of the ways they have been related to through childhood, school, work, and various family and social relationships. One of the powerful opportunities of leadership is to work with staff to light the intrinsic ember of empowerment within them. A spark that says, *I can do this. I have the right and responsibility to do this. I give myself permission.* Without empowerment, staff cannot grow or develop, and no group or organization can reach its potential.

Here are some ideas for both staff and formal leaders: Work together with staff to identify personal and group giftedness (natural strengths). Explore together (one-on-one and in group) staff roles based on their gifts. Minimize punitive approaches to leadership. Role model for staff self-leadership and self-empowerment. Consistently message (personal and group) how and why the group depends on each person's complete contribution. Story-tell (verbally, in writing, through graphic display, and creatively) what empowerment looks, acts, and feels like. Acknowledge and address fears, uncertainties, and insecurities. Get to know each other. Intimacy of relationship reveals and manifests giftedness. Consistently message the importance and benefits of empowerment. Support movement from dependence to independence (from passive student mode to active teacher mode).

Create real time and space for "tribal" gathering, sharing, and connectedness. Celebrate and identify empowerment examples or exemplars. Associate accountability with opportunity and not with potential punishment. Honestly examine fear-based group and organizational history and culture. Encourage and role model productive, caring voice, communication, and feedback. Highlight opportunities to practice empowerment.

In supervisory relationships, it helps to set mutually agreed upon expectations. Otherwise, people feel oppressed and controlled, not empowered. Supervision is not a permission slip for us to beat people down. It is a privilege bestowed, that we lift people up.

When people defer from a duty by saying, "I need training on this. I need to be given skills for this," they might be right. It is also possible that they are copping out, looking for an exit door to get away from accountability. Their statement might also be a form of resisting change. Unless we talk with each other about where such statements are coming from, it is hard to know. Often, people themselves don't know why they say what they say, or what their root feelings are. Explore these roots together.

People can simply be avoidant of the perceived monotony and rigor of practice, and the patience and faith it requires. Critical thinking, problem solving, and deductive reasoning are all muscles. It is necessary that we exercise these muscles through repetition in real-time situations, and in practice scenarios. Don't let people opt out, cop out, or drop out of these practice opportunities. Liven up the growth process by finding creative ways to mark and celebrate progress. Enlist practice partners. Make sure negative self-talk is caringly acknowledged and countered. Provide regular, encouraging feedback.

When staff freeze at making a decision, they are practicing the art of freezing. When facing *decision-paralysis-by-analysis*, have your group ask a question: "What road will get us there?" Will yourselves to choose a road, then take it. Overcome your fear of failure by practicing the taking of roads. When those roads don't work, release them gently. Don't beat yourselves up, just choose another road.

When staff freeze in the face of a situation that needs to be handled, this is a conditioned behavior, a trait of trauma. Maybe past authority figures abused or disempowered them. They are telling themselves a story that causes paralysis. Spend time excavating the stories your staff are telling. Put the paralyzing ones on the table. No, put them in a fire pit and burn them. Have a ceremony. Hoot and holler. Act like wild things now and then. Also, together, create new stories. Ones that tell the truth about the power and ability staff possess. Don't let anyone get away with helplessness stories. Kindly call each other out when they surface. Gradually bring each other back to power.

We all are vulnerable to a fear of negative work outcomes. Letting this fear paralyze us is another matter. Trauma is a culprit in this. As we spend time sharing each other's fear stories, we conspire together to dissolve that fear into fortitude, releasing us from the habit of freezing up when situations barely even suggest difficulty. Growing comfortable with outcomes—whatever they may be—is about learning to invest emotionally not in outcomes but in effort. The way an artist, musician, or athlete strives to do. Outcome fatigue plagues many agencies and professionals. Our cure is to focus on the meaning and reward of the process, and of the moments in which we live.

INVITE THEM

Leaders forever underestimate the degree to which staff feel afraid to ask questions and provide feedback. This is partly because we tend to misunderstand the way people see us in our leadership role. We assume they see us as we see ourselves. But they are imagining us through an authority veil that triggers childhood intimidation and fear in them. The resolution for this? *Continuous invitation.* Welcoming people to share feedback is one thing. They may still feel they would be imposing. Inviting them is a stronger message. It says: "You will be fulfilling my need and desire if you share feedback with me. I will be grateful."

If you have an office, make it inviting for your colleagues or staff. Use the common seductive devices. Candy bowl on your desk. Conversation starters around the room. A stream of sunlight. Essential oil fragrance. Bean bags people can flop onto and be swallowed. Bean bags are great for bringing out the inner child. Also, remember that keeping your door closed sends a message. Not visiting people randomly at their stations sends a message. And having the office that everyone wants to visit sends one of the best messages of all.

In this work of ours, we need to be much more inviting of each other into relationship. So many of us are scared, insecure, hesitant. No matter our age or expertise, we are perpetually the new student at school, waiting to be invited. Invite yourself and your tribe to *feel*, to be whole, to be at your best. Between permission and invitation, we can do great things.

THE IMPORTANCE OF BEING WELCOMED

Have you ever arrived to a social occasion not knowing anyone? A worship service, wedding, class, or even a party? How did that feel? Most of us experience some level of anxiety in the moment. A sense of vulnerability, wariness of the unknown. Emotionally, we need something: for someone to be kind to us. To make us feel welcomed.

Some of the most gifted people in this work are not necessarily more intelligent or informed. They simply make an effort to make others feel welcomed. It is a skill and tool they have practiced, made into habit. They realize that throughout each day, we all have numerous opportunities to make someone feel welcomed. Smiling at another driver. Being warm to the cashier in the checkout line. Greeting people at work, at meetings, in the hallway. Asking about each other, wishing each other well. Showing interest. Listening intentionally. Our facial expressions and body language are powerful determinants of whether someone feels welcomed or unwelcomed by us. We can be powerful hosts or potent *unwelcomers*.

The way we welcome new staff means much. It can set the course for discontent or fulfillment. And not just in new staff, but in the seasoned staff as well. Don't let *business* get in the way of you warmly welcoming new staff. Newness can be a frightening, insecure season. Remember? Make your welcome feel like an invitation, as though you don't know how you all got along before the new person's arrival. It doesn't hurt to make people feel special. It helps.

We tend to assume people are more secure than they are. Swirling in our own insecurities, the whole world appears to us as more secure than we are. But we don't know what our colleague or leader is going through privately, or in the moment. We imagine: *They've shown up for meetings like this a million times. They must feel comfortable at this one.* But a galaxy of change is happening in and around that person, always. Just as for us. It can be a productive practice to assume that everyone you encounter today needs your warm welcome. Welcome them to the moment, the task, the day, the opportunity. Watch your relationships and spaces grow warmer as people feel more at home.

HUMANIZE YOUR STAFF

Staff in a high-stress, high-pace environment are vulnerable to becoming dehumanized, just like people out in the community. Staff dehumanize themselves. They dehumanize each other. And they can be dehumanized by their leadership and agency culture. Following are some starter ideas for working together to ensure that the way staff relate to themselves, and are related to, is humanizing (compassionate, caring, respectful, sensitive, and honoring):

Learn each other's (personal and group) story. Care to be present, pay attention, and read between the lines. Listen to each other's story. People, through their struggles, are always speaking to us. Honor each other's story. The care we take in relationship is how we honor. Celebrate each other's story. Literally celebrate, in the way you choose which stories to retell. Find creative ways of telling. Find kinship. Look for ways that your team shares things in common: mutual states of vulnerability, struggle, instability, "poverty," fear, etc. Use this internally and privately to motivate your sense of kinship, and caring. Avoid judging, resenting, projecting, assuming, or punishing. Correction, discipline, guidance, and support require none of those attitudes. Practice compassion. Not pity, but understanding, appreciation, and sensitivity. See and teach the connection between *seeing* each other and caring for each other. Care for yourself. The more wellness you have, the more humanely you will relate to and treat your peers and teammates. Examine your own triggers and trauma. These are stones in the way of your caring relationship with yourself and each other.

GIVE THEM FOOD AND WATER

Many public agencies, for various reasons, withhold water and food from their staff. Hmmm... It so happens that humans require water and food. Not just for pleasure or extreme survival, but to function. Our brains, hearts, muscles, and electrical circuitry all require not only hydration, but also nutrition. And even when we are not very hungry, healthy snacking can initiate chemical releases that help us manage stress, mood, crisis, and fatigue.

Withholding food and water sends a strong message to staff about how valued or unvalued they are by executive leadership. By their employer. Since we grow thirsty and hungry throughout virtually every day, this means that staff are reminded daily of how their leadership values or fails to value them.

It may cost money to have water fountains in the building. How much money does it cost to have dehydrated workers whose immune systems are more vulnerable, and whose brains are fogged? What is the cost of workers who leave the agency at a higher rate due to a sense of being devalued? We need to become much better at our fiscal accounting of *absence*. The absence of things can affect the bottom line much more than the presence of things (training, resources, salary, etc.).

Sometimes, food and water are synonyms for the human sustenance that staff need to feel valued, appreciated, and worthy. People need to feel this way, and the need is not superficial or the product of selfishness or immaturity. It is core to human wellness. Endless occasions exist in which we can provide even a little food, as a gesture of care. Make sure that feeding your staff food is not a token effort, one not complemented by other forms of nurturing and sustenance. Otherwise your food will be seen as a bandage, and not a genuine act. Food and water should be frosting on the cake of a caring culture.

CORRECTION VERSUS PUNISHMENT

Some believe that correcting staff or service recipients cannot exist hand-in-hand with appreciating them. This is another work tribe myth. We are conditioned to believe that correction should feel much more like a scolding or punishment than like an appreciation. The truth is, correction feeds appreciation. And appreciation makes correction more effective and better received. The two processes are complementary, not contradictory. Practice, and you will see. Compassionate direction feels good to people. Punitive spirit does not. Our climate and culture could use some housekeeping. We need to take stock: How much punitive spirit is being passed around? People who are abused by this spirit are vulnerable to abusing others in the same spirit, and so it goes.

COMPASSIONATE CORRECTION

Even in a corrective job role such as in a Collections Department, we can treat people, and ourselves, with compassion. Holding the people we serve accountable is in fact aided by showing care and compassion. Guilt trips and punitive threats not only trigger and bruise already struggling people, but such energy harms us as a worker if that is the current running through us all day long, day after day. Compassionate correction (or in this case, collection) can be a balm both for the client and the worker. Inquiry can always be done in an appreciative manner. Express that you are inquiring because you care for the person and wish to be of support. Investigation of clientele doesn't have to feel like an interrogation. That is a cultural idea and habit. But the Spanish Inquisition ended long ago.

HUMANIZE THE ONES YOU SERVE

The community's children, youth, and adults who receive agency services have the right, like all of us, to be treated with dignity, respect, compassion, and care. Quantity (quota and compliance) pressure dehumanizes both clients and workers. Social, relational priority rehumanizes these same people. It can be a great challenge for some staff to retain a warm, caring human idea of these vulnerable people. Especially when staff themselves are suffering with stress, unwellness, instability, insecurity; and feelings of being unheard, devalued, not seen, not cared for, and not served or supported. The simple answer to this is to work together with staff to create conditions in which they feel heard, valued, seen, cared for, served, and supported. Here are a few ideas for staff and leaders for humanizing the people you serve. The list is, intentionally, virtually identical to the one for humanizing staff:

Learn their story. Care to be present, pay attention, and read between the lines, even if you only have a sheet of paper or a form from which to gather insight. Listen to their story. People in their struggles are always speaking to us. Honor their story. The care we take in service is the honor we give. Celebrate their story. Literally celebrate, with people and about them, via the storytelling that gets chosen. Find creative ways. Find kinship. Look for ways as staff that you share things in common with those you serve: mutual states of vulnerability, struggle, instability, "poverty," fear, etc. Use this internally and privately to motivate your sense of kinship and caring. Avoid judging, resenting, projecting, assuming, or punishing. Correction, discipline, guidance, and support require none of those attitudes. Practice compassion. Not pity, but understanding, appreciation, and sensitivity. See the connection between "seeing" people and serving them caringly. Care for yourself. The more wellness you have, the more humanely you will relate to and treat people. Examine your own triggers and trauma. These are stones in the way of your caring relationship with people you serve.

FAMILY *ENGAGEMENT*

Staff can role model to those they serve the behaviors and attitudes of healthy relationship: accountability, kindness, patience, Loving speech, compassionate listening. We role model these qualities in the way we treat each other and our clientele. A key part of our treatment has to do with language. For vulnerable, historically devalued service recipients, this term *family engagement* can feel like a military term. Like language originally derived by people who aren't culturally comfortable with the communities they serve. No wonder such language has evolved. Historically, family engagement has been far too hostile, combative, demeaning, and controlling. Families are not wild animals or enemies. They do not need to be engaged. They need to be cared for, learned from, related to. The word *engagement* in some ways reveals the dehumanizing, prejudicial spirit that has plagued system-family relationships.

We are not air-dropping supplies from a battlefield helicopter. *Engagement* implies distance and threat, not closeness and intimacy. It can be a useful term between professionals. Though, for communicating with and marketing initiatives to families, how about we choose more Loving language? Like *family nurturing. Family relations. Family partnering.* Or, *family care.* After all, hurting people want to be treated like family, with all the imperfect intimacy that comes with it.

Ideally, we will become more comfortable immersing ourselves in authentic relationship waters. Staff need support in learning how to nurture the people they serve. Policy and practice guidelines can impede the natural instincts and wisdom of workers. Time is always limited. Workers can feel as though they are spinning in a vortex of priorities, never sure of which priority they should place first. Help them see the connections between the ways they need nurturing, and how their clients may need nurturing. An answer to our service challenges is always within our very own life and nature.

Here is a powerful question we can ask the people we serve: "Please, tell me, how were you able to make this change / accomplish this goal / get through this challenge?" When we ask this question sincerely, we place people in a storyteller/teacher role, empowering them and feeding their healing process. At the same time, we position ourselves to learn, to gather vital information, example, and insight we can share with our colleagues as we together grow in our work and as humans. And, as with any relationship, the healthier we are, the more trusting, intimate, and open we are able to be as we serve. *Serving families like family.* Not a bad motto for an agency.

BE REAL

I have had the awesome, humbling opportunity to *break soul* together with over 200,000 youth worldwide. The majority of these are people who have been seared and shaped by family disruption, homelessness, mental health challenges, adjudication, abandonment, abuse, neglect, and trauma. They are the greatest teachers I have known. We sit together in sacred youth circles and *talk story*, as Indigenous Hawaiian people would say. Many professionals are scared to death of the idea of young people feeling emotions during a formal gathering. I feel strongly, and have learned, that the natural release of suppressed, oppressed emotion in a safe, honoring peer space is one of young people's most powerful medicines. And so, we flow. Using creative self-expression and social affirmation as our tool, youth talk story. They use poetry, spoken word, song, dance, laughter, remembrance, visioning, and tears. So many tears. They share things they have never shared with anyone before. They bathe in each other.

What causes them to feel so safe in these spaces? I feel that much of it has to do with the absence of authority and control-oriented adults. It also helps that the one adult in the circle, me, has cared from the first moment to be emotionally naked with them, particularly in the way I introduce them to my own loss, pain, healing, and journey into self-Love. They feel safe not because they have been told to feel safe, but because they sense the presence of honesty, nakedness, humility, and awe. I sit in awe of them. I share my Love for them with them, right from the start. Many of them have never been outwardly, brazenly Loved before by an adult, never unabashedly embraced by an overflowing heart. Generally, this causes melting, especially of walls. The overflow that then happens is enormous. So full of Grace.

After the sacred circle has concluded, many of these young people approach me, one-by-one. They whisper a consistent message to me: "Jaiya, thank you for being real with us." Regardless of ethnicity, culture, or geographic location, their wording is the same. "Thank you for being real." This tells me that our young people, and hurting people in general, have a deep need for realness. Insincerity and overt procedural behavior and language feels to them like a flagrant trespass. A further wounding. *Being real* cuts through the fear and anxiety, a laser beam that sings silently: *I will not treat you the way so many others have. The true me has come for the true you. You mean that much to me.*

The most fruitful workers and programs are bilingual and bicultural: They speak and write a bureaucratic language that lubricates the machinery and processes of organizations. And they speak and write in the languages of real human beings. This makes people feel safe. As though they are being related to, seen, understood, and honored. Pouring bureaucratic rhetoric over a grieving, frightened human tends not be medicinal. It creates a drought that swallows even workers and formal leaders, as people in the workplace are afraid of being real with each other. *Speaking real* and *being real* are about learning to appropriately shed our rhetorical ways of thinking, feeling, speaking, and acting, and instead communicating with organic humility. *Realness* also requires that we step out from behind our professional masks and dare to reveal our human self, including our story. Not the chronological listing of events in our life, but rather what the real world means to our real heart. It is okay to share our fears, hopes, and lessons learned. In fact, it helps. It fertilizes the soil from which healthy humans grow.

MUTUAL HOMELESSNESS

Transformative servitude requires genuine empathy. The more we can *feel* the lives of others, the more we are flooded with understanding. Without understanding, service provision becomes colonizing. Imposing. Harmful. Fortunately, we can grow understanding by focusing on kinship. Kinship between us and those we serve. We start by reflecting on the realities of their lives, and on their suffering and beauty. In terms of their suffering, our systems have categorized various plights: *Homelessness. Mental Illness. Poverty. Unemployment. Incarceration. Foster care.* If we can look through these labels and gaze the realities within, we find entry points to discovering what we have in common with target populations.

Take homelessness. We interpret this term to refer to the absence of consistent, viable shelter. If we look deeper, though, we see that *psychological homelessness* is at the root of physical homelessness. If you help take a person off the streets and place them in a mansion without addressing their underlying challenges, their psychological homelessness, soon enough the person will be back on the streets. Resources, then, are not a person's primary need, nor should they be a system's primary objective. We are learning to go from pushing systems to healing systems. In a healing system, we address and treat root causes.

We empower our ability to treat root causes by identifying with the root. What is our kinship with psychological homelessness? Each of us, in every level of the system, has personal experience with psychological homelessness, including discontent in relationships, jobs, roles, rewards, etc. If our system cultures encouraged this exploration, seeing this form of kinship as a fundamental practice tool, we would grow adept at identifying our kinship points and using them to create relationship, safe spaces, insight, and powerful intuition. We would achieve, in relation to communities and coworkers, a useful sense of mutual homelessness. A state of awareness and sensitivity that strengthens bonds, sheds shame associations with the term *homeless*, and increases our ability to address physical homelessness.

MUTUAL POVERTY AND JOBLESSNESS

Identifying the ways in which we have experienced *various poverties* in our life (relationship, health, wellness, etc.) can help us relate to families, children, and coworkers in a spirit of kinship, and increase our sensitivity to the nature and impact of poverty in general. Poor physical and mental health, loneliness, despair, negativity, devaluation, low morale, burnout, and mediocre work are all forms of inner poverty. Also, if we are not in meaningful touch with our gifts, purpose, or calling, we are in a very real sense *jobless* even if we are earning a paycheck. This is a spiritual, emotional, mental joblessness that leaves us deprived of a sense of place and value and worth. These kinds of psychological poverty and joblessness are opportunities for us to relate to the struggles and suffering of community members and coworkers. Within our own impoverishment and dislocation we may activate and receive a very real sense of kinship, empathy, humility, sensitivity, and support. When this happens, we come alive with a spirit of mutual care and inspired servitude.

MUTUAL HEALING

We have all been wounded, hurt, and traumatized in our life. We respect the healing journeys of others by honoring our own healing journeys, and supporting each other in a spirit of ongoing healing, growth, and improvement. At work, groups often come together to heal their collective wounds only to create more wounding. This happens when we are careless with language, tone, and emotion. There is a difference between venting and releasing. When we vent, we are practicing trauma. This deepens despair and fills people and the environment with toxicity. When we release we are practicing the healing of trauma. The difference is a matter of tone, intent, and spirit. Venting carries toxin, so it poisons and destroys. Releasing carries hope and peace, so it heals. We can move our group from venting to releasing by holding each other accountable, communicating constructively, and developing self-nurturing skills.

HOMEFULNESS

If psychological homelessness is a dysfunctional state, there must be a corresponding state on the functional end of the same continuum. We can call this *homefulness*. The Vietnamese Buddhist Monk Thich Nhat Hanh was exiled by his government from his beloved homeland during what we call the Vietnam War. He was exiled for leading his fellow monks in practicing peace outside of the monastery walls, in communion with their surrounding communities. *Thay*, as his students call him, soon grew despondent at the thought of never returning to Vietnam. He mourned the loss of family, friends, familiar food and customs, the fragrance of spring blossoms, all that he had known.

Thay came to realize that he had talked himself into a state of psychological, spiritual homelessness. Although he was already regarded as a spiritual teacher worldwide, he had created within himself a traumatized climate of loss. Then, Thay had a wonderful illumination: As long as he was true to himself, then no matter where in the world he found himself, no matter who he was around, he would be truly home. With this recognition, and the practice of being *at home*, he achieved what we can call homefulness. He freed himself from the disruption and counter-productivity of feeling as though he didn't belong. He empowered himself, by practiced attitude alone, into his giftedness to be peace, teach peace, and garden peace.

We too can achieve homefulness in our work. It is necessary, or else we are courting stress, anxiety, fear, doubt, and ultimately atrophy as professionals and systems. With attention to our sense of belonging within our roles and within our teams and tribes, we can activate an entitlement of inspiration, creativity, health, and efficacy. We can practice belonging in our work, and in our relationships with each other. Belonging in turn unleashes our greatest version: faithful, secure, attuned, and thriving.

FREAKING OUT IS CONTAGIOUS

Remember, no matter how many people are freaking out around you, you are not required by law to freak out. Freaking out is contagious because of the mirror cells in our brain and nervous system that make us such impressionable, social creatures. We are designed to mimic and imitate. In a primal way, this is what helps us learn, from birth, from our social world about how to survive and thrive. But when our mirror cells become misappropriated by fear, stress, and anxiety, they begin to serve an unhealthy function. Our mimicry reflex now causes us to join panic and anxiety when we are exposed to it. We become like kindling at the foot of a forest fire, igniting in a flash, feeding the fire as it spreads through our workplace. *No bueno.* To develop resistance to this *freaking out* contagion, first, take good care of yourself as a preventative measure. Second, practice being aware of what in your environment you are mimicking. Catch yourself when you mimic panic and anxiety. Develop a taste for mimicking calm and centeredness. It does exist in people and in nature around you. Talk with your colleagues regularly about your collective effort not to freak out. Together, you are developing immunity against freaking out. Your journey is a story you can continue sharing, as a muscle-building exercise. Eventually, you will be strong enough to stay inside of curative peace during the daily storms that come with social and workplace turbulence.

BE A MODERATOR AND A MEDIATOR

In the presence of rage, Love is as a dousing rain.
In the presence of crisis, calm is a divine balm...

We can either increase or decrease the *magnitude* of the stress, panic, chaos, and negativity we encounter at work. This is what I mean by the act of *moderating*. We do this by being mindful of how we prepare for, receive, process, and react to what others bring us, and to how they bring it to us. Being a moderator requires that we consciously determine that we will be a human workplace filter through which positivity becomes pronounced and negativity diminished. We literally change the intensity of another person's energy in a healthy direction.

Being a *mediator* involves us changing the *quality* of the energy we encounter from negative to positive and purposeful. We can change negative, panicked energy that others bring us into positive, calm energy, simply by being aware of our power to do so, and by giving ourselves the permission to do so. As we choose to be calm, we role model others into calmness. Through our compassionate listening and attention, we soothe them. We remind them to breathe, and prompt them to change perspectives. Reminding them of the larger picture, and of their own power, can help them to will their panic, anxiety, or combativeness into a certain peace. Remind them of their true nature, and of their power to manage situations. Mediation is a craft, so practice and behold the harvest.

It is possible for us to both moderate and mediate in the same moment. When someone approaches you with conflict, complaint, or panic, smile brightly at them and say, "I Love you." That's it. Three words that may cause them to seek therapy, but that might also shock them into a calm sucking of the thumb, like a baby. After all, those three words have been soothing us since birth. You can also find your own language and ways to diffuse and transform energy coming from others or yourself.

Some things insulate us from toxic, dysfunctional attitudes, behaviors, and stories. Other things aggravate the same variables. True self-care and mindfulness is an insulating factor. Self-neglect is an aggravating factor. You can come up with your own list, and it may be useful to do so, as a way of keeping in touch with the nature of your workplace landscape.

Overreacting and underreacting are two social behaviors that greatly influence group wellness and mood. Reflect on your own triggers, things that cause you to lose your composure and act outside of your true nature. Have your group reflect on the same. Do this together and privately. The more you share and talk about triggers, the more you help each other grow desensitized to those stimuli. Calmness becomes a climate you grow together. Calmness is a powerful response to trauma, crisis, panic, and stress. It is a potent example and role model. It is a teaching spirit. And it creates the conditions most optimal for addressing difficult situations. No rule says we are not allowed to remain calm as we serve crisis. Being calm when others are not is one of the great leadership traits and tools.

REMEMBERING PEACE

The Nepalese have a saying: *Shanti ko Samjhana. Remembering Peace.* This idea and its practice are at the heart of how we may remain well as we journey through work and life. We remember peace when we practice traveling in our thoughts to those moments in our life when we were simply feeling good. This returns us to our true, relaxed, creative, free, self-permissive nature. It opens us and empowers us to *BE* that peace within any storm. *Remembering Peace* is not just a habit. It is a personality we cultivate. The more time we spend in peace, the more its nature is reflected in our own.

REFRAME THE CRISIS

Even the most challenging, painful situation does not by law have to be defined as crisis within our heart and mind. We have the power to redefine any situation as an opportunity to serve, as a chance to stretch and grow and apply what we have learned. How we define a situation invites either stress hormones or peace hormones to flood our body and our brain. Put out false fires. People will frantically work to convince you that a situation is a cataclysmic disaster, when in truth it is not. When this happens, don't be the one fanning the flames of a false fire. Be the one who brings calm and perspective and throws water on the false fire to put it out.

FLOW

The foundation of wellness is flow. During my priceless opportunity to study Tibetan Holistic Medicine while living in Nepal, I received subtle insights from practitioners that I find useful to this day. I sat at the feet of these sages as they graciously poured out their insight to me like plentiful cups of *dud chia* (milk tea). They told me, "Jivan (my Nepali name), we define health and wellness as energy in motion. We define illness and disease as energy blocked. Everything, then, is a matter of flow. Where you find flow, encourage and preserve it. Where you find flow blocked, learn to release the blockage. Help people to know how to remove their own obstructions, and to preserve their own flow."

For the Tibetan doctors, every aspect of life can be distilled down into this matter of flow. From family life, to relationships of all kinds, to learning in school and in the world. For them, flow is at the heart of all that happens in the body, mind, heart, and spirit. It is the fabric of wellness in any group, community, organization, or society. And what is it that opens flow? Communication. Honesty. Truth. Compassion. Love. Listening. Receiving. Giving. Remembering. Breathing. Laughing. Crying. Grieving. Celebrating. *How flow can you go?*

Flow is good because it carries sediment out of us, leaving us open and fertile for the good things that wait to flow into us. This is the nature of a river. Systems, and people, are rivers, too. Obstructions block our flow, keeping us from growing, and causing regression and fermentation. This is true for workers, leaders, and work tribes. Flow acts by continuously breaking down and removing obstructions before they become too solid or large. Organizations stay alive by virtue of vascular systems that must be kept clear and flowing. Healthy relationships and the stories they produce are that vascularity.

ROOT OBSTRUCTIONS TO SELF-CARE

Self-care is a popular topic these days. A fad, if you will. Care systems can end up wed to fad-based funding streams. If they are not careful, these systems become led by fads and not as much by vision and inspiration. Being allegiant to fads, though, causes us to miss opportunities for true change. These opportunities exist down deep, beneath the surface level at which fads operate. For example, we all know the popular modes of self-care. We've been socialized to death on the modes: deep breathing, yoga, tantric this and that, nutrition, spas, manicures and pedicures, salt and mud baths, exotic fruit facials... you know the species we're talking about here.

Our issue is not a lack of knowledge, but a lack of action. What is keeping us from self-care? This can be a more valuable question to ask than the question of modes and methods. Deep in each of us are obstructions. Often from childhood. Seeds of thought, belief, or emotion that keep us from taking care of ourselves. We may identify guilt as a big seed. But even guilt is not necessarily a root obstruction. Guilt is more likely a gaseous emanation arising from a deeper, more imbedded obstruction. Such as a conversation we had, something someone told us, a brief encounter, or a chronic exposure. If we follow the river back to its origin, we arrive at its source. Guilt is not the source. It is the breath of the source.

Once we identify sources, they require that we stay with them consistently enough to dissolve their solidity. *Rainmakers.* That's what we need to become in treating our obstructions. Even light rainfall of healing thought and attention over time can break down these cysts of the psyche. Thought is medicine. Thought that generates emotion and energy counter to that of the obstruction. So, no more swimming on the surface inside of fads. Time for the deep diving and the discoveries down there that introduce us to our obstructions. Every single thing you do to Love and care for yourself is an example to your colleagues. Someone is always watching. Let them see you being good to you, being true to you, being you. Caring for each other also sets a great example. People are watching for this, too. At its heart, caring for yourself is a continuous river of decisions: choices to route and reroute your thoughts toward Love, healing, and growth. Fear, doubt, and worry can be self-abusive. Erasing. Polluting. Self-care is a deep, habitual river in the soul that says, "I will not harm this sacredness I am."

THE POURING

All day long you get poured into. By people. Cases. Encounters. Authority. Crisis and tragedy. Loss and grief. Pain and uncertainty. Healing, hope, and triumph. Love and caring. Every day. It's that every day part that sets your work apart. Continuous, full, flagrant, fragrant pouring. What do you do with what gets poured into you? This is a question at the heart of caring for yourself. Where do you put it? Where does it go? What does it do inside of you?

You have your own ways of managing the pouring. Ways you have developed over time. Many of those ways may have originated in childhood. Have you examined your ways since then? Doing so is a good first step in managing the pouring. Recognizing that you have been poured into is another good initial step. Know that anything that gets poured into must be poured out of, or it becomes full, overflowing. Basic principle, often neglected. Reflect on your release modes and valves. Do they work? Are they rusted or blocked?

Here is a simple way to think about it: *Make sure that your outflow is greater than your inflow.* This will keep you available for more flow. Make sure also that what flows into you is touched by your sincere attention. As you touch it, you can mindfully transform it into the energy you need. Create compost. Generate fertile soil. Then release what you need to. You have endless available ways to create outflow. Anything that moves you emotionally, spiritually, or mentally, prompts you to open and release. If you feel that you don't know how to open and release, it is more likely that you haven't been practicing. Or you do release but don't realize it. Spend time with yourself and become familiar with your ways of release.

ADVOCATE FOR YOUR WELLNESS

I am using the term *advocate* many times, for a reason. If you look at historical change movements and at smaller, uncelebrated change processes, you can see that *to advocate* does not mean to ask for something one time and then give up. Advocacy is a persistent rainfall and drumbeat. It requires persuasion and growth over time, sometimes decades or centuries. The old "I asked them and they told me *no,*" line that can accompany disempowerment and helplessness is not enough. Advocacy works, but like servitude, advocacy is a long and faithful endeavor. In fact, there is no convenient passage of time after which we get to accurately say, "We advocated and it didn't work."

Trauma causes us to shrink inside ourselves. From there, we wait passively like children for someone to save us. If we feel someone is not advocating for us the way we want, that person becomes a target for our venom. As we spew venom, we fail to do anything to actually advocate. Advocacy is not attack. The two are frequently confused. But if you meet attack on the street, you will know it by its ugly face and by the ugly way it makes you feel. Advocacy is a more beautiful soul. Advocacy is not a selfish striving. It is a spirit of mutual care. When you advocate for yourself, you are buoyed by a Love for yourself, a desire that you be well. And also by a care for your tribe, a yearning that you all be well.

Advocating for wellness in an unwell system can be like convincing a lion to play nicely with a gazelle. Be aware that you will be swimming upstream against the current. Being aware and prepared fortifies you for the swim. You will not always have allies *Amening* your every breath. Advocate anyway. When you encounter doubt or ridicule, take this as evidence of the unwellness against which you have chosen to advocate. You have stirred sediment in the fetid pond. Let these reactions motivate and renew your cause. In a hateful space, Love is scorned. So it goes for trying to be well in a spoiled place. Do not be discouraged. Resistance is the first sign that you are on to something good.

CATCH AND RELEASE... AND CATCH

We can learn to catch the good things. Picture a child running through a wildflower field with net, chasing butterflies. This is a good strategy for being well: *Learn to catch the beautiful things.* Not to possess them. To become them. We can become skilled at catching positive stories, helpful strategies, and healthful habits, and releasing or sharing them with the tribe. We aren't very good right now at feeding each other. We can be. It is our nature. Instead of hoarding what comes to us, or what we gather, we can grow into a passion for releasing it onward. That is what it came to us for in the first place: to end up as a meal for the masses. This way, the good stuff doesn't die in us, like a living thing caught and released in the ocean, the good things we share go on living. At the same time, the act of releasing, or sharing, creates a relational vitality that causes others to share with us. We end up catching more fish (work food) than what we shared. This is fruitful mathematics. Abundance works this way.

BREATHING WORKS

Deep, full breathing is a miraculous tonic. It opens everything in us that needs to be opened. It floods the brain and body with nourishing blood flow. Just as we were designed to sweat to release toxins, we were designed to breathe, in no small part to release natural tension. Deep breathing, in our highly changed work, releases tremendous amounts of tension and stress; and calms the heart, nerves, and mind. And yet, it is the last thing many of us pay attention to during our workday. It should be the first. We don't believe in its power because we are impressionable creatures and no one around us in our unwell culture seems to be breathing. Not our own family or friends, not coworkers or leaders. So we figure, *this breathing thing must be overrated.* But how's that working for us?

For those of us who are uncomfortable considering an idea without statistics, rest assured, the research is considerable and decisive. Effective breathing reduces stress and anxiety, decreases inflammatory cortisol and adrenaline, increases calming serotonin and oxytocin, improves memory and mood, diminishes depression, improves prosocial behavior, increases cognitive performance, combats fatigue; and energizes the body, spirit, and mind. Maybe breathing is a work resource? Too crazy? Breathe on it.

GRIEVE

True grieving is not a pitiful, destructive act. It is an act of healing. It is a form of flow. Of release. Of healing. Systems that don't hold space and permission for grieving become depressed places of chronic, unreleased grief. Serving human lives involves grief. Working with others in this cause brings more grief. People change their positions, are promoted, leave the job. Formal leaders transition away. Those left behind feel abandoned, even lost. We grieve these various relationships and their influence, which is a good thing. A reflection of the meaning the relationships have to us. A testimony to the bonds and journey. Healthy grieving celebrates the memories, even the challenging ones. It is a storytelling river that goes on for years. Our relationships become legend, and in becoming legend, serve as mortar for the foundation of a relational system.

We can grieve any and all change, granular or grandiose. If we move into a new office, we grieve the old one. We grieve the old staff meeting schedule. The old office building, or route to work. The stops we used to make in our day. Past families with whom we worked. Past leadership. Old policies, laws, practices. Change can be a tender, poignant thing if we nurture each other in grieving. If not, change quickly grows harsh, cold, punishing. Grieving is not a distraction from work. Grieving together, as a tribe, makes life and work a warmer river.

Grief is natural and seasonal. Trauma lies to us, telling us that grief is the end of the world and never-ending. For healthy grieving in this work that brings us human pain, we need to address our trauma. Otherwise grief grows out of control in us. It goes from being a river of healing to a tornado of torment and despair. Nurture the trauma and we allow grief to do its divine work in us.

So grieve. Grieve your favorite blend of coffee no longer available in the break room. The initiative you gave so much to, only to see its leaders exit and new leaders arrive with their own priorities. Your old office with the window that let in actual sunlight. The fragrance your former coworker used to wear. Your old pencils and pens. Your old laptop. The wardrobe that went out of style even though you kept wearing it long after. Grieve it all. In your own private ways. And together, with the only people in your life who may fully understand your wild work: your fellow servant tribe.

CRYING IS A TOOL

Crying can be a great stress and management tool. It releases not only tears, but also stress-reducing chemicals in the body. Muscles sigh and grow fluid after crying. Ever notice that sensation we might call *a crier's high*, after you have let it all out? This is a true high, caused by the pain relieving hormones that like to party after we cry. Of course, we are trained by society and profession not to be emotional. Let me correct that. We are trained not to cry. We are encouraged to be emotional, absolutely. Certain emotions, such as anger, combativeness, fuming, resentment, sadness, melancholy, grimness, and frustration seem to be socially encouraged in the workplace.

When people cry, there is no need to have a panic attack. They are simply releasing stress and pressure. They are washing their interior of toxicity, abating trauma. If we can grow accustomed to crying in the same way we are with laughter, this may be a very helpful practice. I am not referring to histrionics, by the way. Not drama shows. Rather, crying as meditative device, as breathing can be. In fact, forms of motion and flow, like tai chi, are kindred spirits to crying. Both move things through us and out of us, leaving us in a flushed, post-spa bliss.

LAUGH MEDICINE

Laughter changes everything. Research shows how powerful a medicine it is for the one who is laughing. But laughter is also like a happy gas for the social environment. Laughter immediately affects the cognitive and neurological systems of people in the vicinity. It travels an intimate energetic tether between bodies, charging the air. It isn't only contagious, it is invasive. Its disseminating energy moves into us, immediately unraveling our tension knots and solemn mood. Laughter is a masseuse. It is so powerful, it can override even our most painful moments and force us to join the party, even if only for a precious moment.

If laughter is this powerful, it may benefit us as workers, leaders, and tribes to take laughter seriously as a system resource. As a rehabilitative tool. Who are the clowns in your court? This is a good question to ask. Are these people, these natural laughter fountains, being positioned within the environment to become *Johnny Laughterseeds*? Are they being encouraged and celebrated in their laugh giftedness? Their presence and persona can be as healing to a group as a clinical therapist, and you don't even have to pay for it. These human laugh factories just want to be set free to inspire laughter. Let them run with it, and their technical work is likely to improve, as is the work of everyone around them. Immune systems will be strengthened and you may see fewer sick days. This isn't fantasy. The research on laughter is serious...

Humor is one of our greatest practical tools for managing trauma and maintaining wellness. It is a sacred human quality, in fact. We need to invest in creating cultures of laughter, light-heartedness, and humor. This does not disrespect the challenges our service recipients face. Rather, it empowers and fortifies us to be well as we support them. Stress is rampant in this work. To counteract this, we require daily flushing of harmful energy. Whether through laughter, tears, hugs, meditation, walks, storytelling, deep breathing, or other methods, each of us can find our most natural ways of flushing negative, traumatizing energy from our bodies, minds, and emotions. And, of course, practice makes this constant cleansing a habitual hum and grace.

MINDFULNESS

I use the term *mindfulness* in this book, so we should pause and reflect on its meaning. Mindfulness is yet another culturally appropriated concept. It is popularly used now, almost always out of context, which is what cultural appropriation does. It wants you to believe that an idea didn't exist until the dominant culture *discovered* it. This serves to bolster the supremacy campaign of the dominant culture, while dehumanizing the culture from which the idea or tradition originated. I mention this because cultural appropriation does great damage to the relationship between helping systems and communities, and between helping professionals and the people they serve. In the case of mindfulness, the idea has been severed from its cultural roots to such a degree that many believe it is the epiphany of some enlightened class of mainstream modern sages.

Mindfulness is deeply rooted in the ancient traditions of meditation found in many spiritual practices. Its true meaning is not to simply be aware, but to be in touch with the divine goodness that is *all things*. To be not just intellectually awake, but alive in the heart and soul, alive to the oneness of life. Mindfulness is a state of being that immerses us in the compassion's stream. This makes mindfulness salient in this book. And perhaps the word *mind* in the term *mindfulness* causes many to misunderstand what parts of our *being* are at play. Not just the mind. Our whole *being*, with mind as a tool for activating an openness through which we experience emptiness. *Emptiness*. Not the absence of things, but the presence of *presence*. In that the nature of *presence* is compassion, mindfulness is a tool for our compassion work. We are compassion workers. But only fully so when we are in a state of authentic, soulful mindfulness. The more we succumb to stress, anxiety, fear, and imbalance, the greater our detachment from the compassion so vital in our work.

AFTER THE PAINFUL MOMENT

We need moments, spaces, and processes that allow us to reintegrate with our true nature after a difficult, painful moment. Immediately after, when possible. We need a culture that encourages us to take a deep breath after putting down the phone from a trauma-filled conversation. We need skilled counselors in the office, especially peer counselors, who can help us not just debrief but also decompress, detoxify, and calm our inflammatory hormones. We need someone to talk with who can understand what we were just exposed to. We need a hug. We need to cry. We need to laugh it off. We need support systems. We carry great guilt over tragic or unfortunate case outcomes. We need to grieve.

In our own way, and together. We also have a human need to share the story that just emerged into our life.

PEACEFUL PAUSE

We are learning how to care for ourselves, gradually humbling ourselves enough to learn from our ancient grandparent cultures: The same ones we have dismissed as uncivilized, undeveloped, *third world*, and primitive. One lesson we are learning is that after a difficult moment, it is helpful to pause. Emergency room teams are learning to take a brief, unrushed moment simply to stand together in silence and reverence after a patient dies in their hands. This peaceful pause before moving onto the next critical patient blesses each person's holistic health, strengthens the team, and makes their work with the next patient more effective.

This peaceful pause does not cost time, it saves it. Workers are calmer, centered. The brief pause and giving of reverence is a natural part of our need to grieve, or simply decompress. Too many of us are rushing from horror to tragedy to crisis to conflict without ever pausing to fully breathe once during our day. Then we jump in the car and head home, absolutely traumatized. Now, though, we are alone, separated from our colleagues who might best empathize with our trauma. Try a peaceful pause with your coworkers. Try it after the hard moments. Try pausing to begin and conclude your staff meetings. At the beginning and end of your workday. In this critically ill world of rushing and panic, learn to trust in the power of pausing. Discover the peace that grows in that meadow.

AN ENCOURAGING WORD

An encouraging word, from a leader or a colleague, even in an email, text, or social media post (be covert) can do wonders for the soul. We vastly underestimate the power of brief encouragement. Take yourself, for instance: How many times have you been having a hard day, only to have someone be kind to you in a brief moment? Remember feeling as though the gesture changed your whole day? Remember the rush of endorphins, the good feeling moving through you? Your instant change in attitude and mood? Like kindness, encouragement has this power. Use it. Never stop using it. It is one of your intrinsic tools, no permission slip or employer provision necessary.

INTEGRATE THE WHOLE OF YOU

If you segregate yourself too much into fractions, each fraction will eventually fall apart. Your work self is not actually separate from your personal self. It is built upon the foundation of your personal self. Segregating the two is a psychology rooted in the illusion that you can be divided. The effort leads to suffering, stress, and dysfunction. If you do not wish to be *dys*functional, stop *dissing* your functional self! Your functional self is an aspect of your wholeness, not your fractions. Staying in touch with your whole self is an art, a craft, a... you guessed it: wholesome practice.

ACKNOWLEDGE YOUR CONDITIONS

It helps to learn how to acknowledge, without judgment, our external and internal conditions. To not be so afraid of the truth of them. For they exist and impact us continuously, regardless of our acknowledgment. But in denial, those conditions have free reign over our wellness and productivity. With honest attention, we can transform some conditions and adapt in a healthful manner to others. Grow comfortable with taking stock of your inner state. Treat the act like self-blessing. Because it is one.

THE PRICE WE PAY FOR CLOSING

When we close, we suffer. This is how we are designed. We think of closing as protective. It is not protective, it is reactive. It is survival. At first. Soon, any closing becomes destructive, because we were made to be open. Breathing is a great example of this. Sometimes, we feel the valid need to hold our breath, maybe when we are underwater. Eventually, though, if we do not breathe, we die. You may think: *But what if I am always underwater when it comes to work? If I stop holding my breath, I will drown.* Clever thinking, my friend. The problem here is that it only *feels* like you are underwater at work. This is a grand illusion. The truth is, you may be in a difficult work environment, but you are in fact in an atmosphere of air. If you breathe, you will not drown. You will live. It is in your literal and figurative breath-holding that you are truly drowning.

Closing takes many tolls, including the loss of social intimacy and its benefits: support, decreased stress, and sense of belonging. Also: the loss of social feedback about our work and various challenges. Absence of acknowledgement, appreciation, and celebration of our work triumphs. Increased blood pressure. Declines in emotional, mental, and physical health. The list continues... Whatever causes us to close, closing itself magnifies and intensifies that harmful element. The hurt bounces around inside of us, causing further damage, and in some cases growing in that darkness of neglect.

THE GIFT OF OPENING

Opening is not just an act. It is a precursor to wellness. It is like opening windows in your home to let in the fresh air. Opening allows both the goodness and hurt in us to flow out. It allows fresh energy, Love, caring, support, and relational fertility to flow into us. Opening is a way of flushing out stress and work toxicity. It allows us to be infused with social nutrition, insights, and feedback.

Being open is not primarily for the sake of others. It benefits *us* first and foremost. Openness is a choice. A best practice. Maybe we are afraid that being open allows hurt to come in. But hurtfulness hurts regardless of our relational posture. It is an illusion to believe that being closed softens blows of hurtfulness. This is a story we tell ourselves without deeply examining the truth.

A system's spirit of openness or closedness is a function of the openness and closedness of each employee. Environment is not determined by work outcomes, though this seems to be the notion that drives our worried scurrying. Whether service experiences are difficult or promising, if workers and leaders assume a habitually closed persona, this becomes the energy that employees and community feel. This matters. A system's energy allows it to be a source of healing in a community. This energy can also be a source of continuing collective hurt.

WHAT OPENS US

We know that sunlight opens a flower. We also know what opens and closes a human being, though we spend little time reflecting on this as workers and leaders. As a result, systems evolve climates that create opening and closing without any intention on the part of the people in those climates.

Here is an exercise that any worker or formal leader can use personally and within the group: Simply reflect on the relationships of your life. Personal. Romantic. Friendship. Classmates and teachers. Teammates. Coworkers. Take your heart back to central moments in each of these relationships. Ask yourself two questions: *What qualities in my relationships have made me feel safe?* And, *what qualities in my relationships have made me feel unsafe?* Write your answers in two lists. Be honest with yourself. Even painfully honest. You are not doing this for social presentation purposes. You are doing it to know yourself better. And to empower your awareness.

Whatever you write down as qualities that make you feel safe is now the first draft of what will be your ongoing blueprint or best practice paradigm for how to treat people in your work, and how you require others to treat you. You are the greatest authority when it comes to your own list. You don't need to attend a seminar or training, read a book, or earn a degree. Just keep returning to your list, reconsidering it, refining, polishing, evolving as your experiences evolve. The beauty of this practice is that whatever relationship qualities make you feel safe or unsafe, are likely to make all other human beings with whom you interact also feel safe or unsafe: those you serve, coworkers, formal leaders. This is because you are a human being and they are human beings. When it comes to feeling safe or unsafe, regardless of our differences, on a primal level we are remarkably kindred.

Use this self-check technique whenever you or your team or tribe encounter conflict, disagreement, crisis, uncertainty, stress, or a need to change. Remember that personal intention is not an excuse for hurtfulness. Ask yourselves: "How are we making each other feel? How do we hold each other? Warmly, in a way that feels good? Or like porcupines, so that even when we try to embrace each other, it feels like sharp quills sinking into our hearts?" Through honest, honoring conversation, get at the heart of how your group culture touches its members. Then, garden your ways.

Feeling safe is a primary need for people in order to open. If we are asking a coworker, supervisee, or ourselves to make any kind of change, much more receptiveness will occur when people feel safe. Safety is primary in the psychology of change. Not information. Safety. We all need safe spaces to breathe and work. And, importantly, to reflect on the work. Reflection is not a lazy departure from the work. It is the ground from which inspired, aware, sensitive work grows. For a space to feel safe, it also needs to feel non-punitive. It needs to feel open-minded, open-hearted, and nonjudgmental. It can't feel hurried, frantic, or anxious. You know what peace feels like. Include peace in your safety construction designs.

WHAT CLOSES US

Whatever causes us to open also causes us to close when it is absent. Examining the absence of opening factors is a way to figure out the way forward for personal and group change. If we want workers or service recipients to feel and act more empowered, or formal leaders to be more sensitive, honoring, or responsive, we can first look at what absences they are experiencing that are causing them to close. When rehabilitating any system, identifying the absence of opening factors needs to occur at the beginning, along with identifying the presence of closing factors. Once we know what is missing, we can figure out how to make it present. Once we realize what needs to be gone, we can find a way to get rid of it. Just keep in mind, this kind of creativity requires that people feel safe enough to create the always evolving blueprint. Social safety forever seems to be a group's foundational need.

WALK IT OUT

Getting up from your desk and simply walking is one of the most underappreciated best practices for managing stress, maintaining health, and problem solving. Walking is a form of opening, just as is breathing. Walking awakens the body, gets your blood to flow, and releases calming and clarifying hormones. Walking brings a natural breeze against your face and skin, which stimulates serenity and creativity. Walking is a rhythmic act (ironically preventing arrhythmia), which is also calming and good for reflective thought. Walking can help dissipate anger, frustration, fear, and fatigue.

We aren't just talking about laps around a high school running track. Benefits happen even when walking around the cubicles or office, or briefly stepping outside to walk around the building. Walking is one of the best *friends with benefits*. It is free, doesn't have to take long, and you don't need to change into your gym clothes. Walking also helps with digestion, circadian rhythm (especially for those of you who travel a lot), internal inflammation, memory, mood, and optimism. You may feel that you are short on resources in your work, but at least rest content with knowing that one resource is imminently available. Just like breathing, walking (or other forms of mobility) is yours to use. Walk it out.

IDENTITY ASSESSMENT

It can be useful to ask ourselves: *Who am I?* Then compare the answer with the answer we get from asking: *Who have I come to believe I am?* We can ask these two questions of both our personal and professional self, which surely overlap. Let us continuously take stock in the story inside of us that defines who we believe ourselves to be. This story, our identity, is the root of how we exist in the world. Our conditions don't shape our lives nearly as much as our idea of who we are. This practice work can be done personally and as a team. *Who-work* can be a pleasurable practice, a passionate private art.

NURTURE YOUR TRIGGER POINTS

Being aware of our sensitive trigger points is a first step in learning to manage those sensitivities, so that we aren't helplessly reacting to everything and everyone around us. Trigger points can be nurtured and healed. By showering these points with Loving attention, we transform them. They grow from being volatile landmines into being tender places that simply need ongoing care. Explosiveness comes from unattended wounds. Our choice to make our workplace a nonexplosive atmosphere means that we have wounds to tend. In doing so, we renew our work.

ENJOY THE MOMENT

Trauma in us causes us to be tense and anxious, anticipating that the sky is going to fall at any moment. We may tell ourselves a story: *In this work, the sky is always falling.* This causes us to physiologically experience a falling sky even when things are calm. Even as we eat, sleep, vacation, or reflect. It helps not to anxiously anticipate the next crisis. Enjoying calm moments completely is a skill that needs practice. No magical tool. Just work to become calm inside of calmness. And whatever you are good at savoring—wine, food, intimacy, sunset or moonrise—transfer those savoring sensations to the delicacy of your present moments. Learn to taste them fully on your palate of joy.

REVIEW DAILY HOW YOU TREAT YOURSELF

Life and culture cause us to beat ourselves up, judge and blame ourselves, and to neglect ourselves. Continuously check-in to see how, honestly, you are treating yourself. Whatever you discover, be gentle with what you find. Simply resolve to treat yourself better. Conduct ceremonial burnings of your bad habits. Artistically surround your workspace with reminders of your good habits. Affirmation seeds inspiration. You can become your most wonderful masseuse.

MAKE YOUR MIND A SPA

Our mind is an accumulation of thoughts, a patterned constellation of ideas. The more Loving, caring, forgiving, and nurturing our thoughts, the more our mind becomes like a spa we can visit, for free, at any time to receive massage, renewal, pampering, relaxation, and respite. Like any spa, your mind needs to be cleaned and maintained. Use the cleaning tools and solutions that suit you: prayer, meditation, visualization, mantras, singing, solitude, quietude, a good quick nap... You know your bag of tricks. Use everything inside.

GIVE YOURSELF PERMISSION

It is amazing how often we as adults do not give ourselves permission to be well. All the oppressive relationships of our childhood are still with us, inner voices that tell us what we can and cannot do. No matter how many degrees or titles we have, if we haven't healed that childhood wound of oppression, we have a hard time existing in freedom, yes? Practice giving yourself permission. Permission to be happy, to smile, to be Loving at work. Permission to express yourself, to say no, to question something that concerns you. Permission simply to ask for permission, which some people rarely do, so complete is their fear paralysis. You will know a healthy workplace by the fertile hum of adults giving themselves the gift of permission.

EMBRACE YOUR GIFTS

Our giftedness brought us to this work, to this calling. But because our giftedness is so infinite and powerful, often we become afraid of it. It suggests to us that we have infinite capacity to do our work. Which means that we then have to take responsibility for our work instead of passing it off to someone else "above" us, saying, "I don't have the skills for this." This attitude, honestly, is the product of fear and avoidance. We are trying to find an easy way out. We tell ourselves we are too small, which we feel is our ticket out of having to stretch and grow and meet the challenge. Instead, we can overcome our fear and embrace the truth that we are gigantic, powerful, and fully capable, exactly because we are gifted for this work. We didn't arrive here randomly. We arrived on a blazing comet of purpose. Let us exist accordingly.

TAKE OFF YOUR ARMOR

For many of us, from the moment we first wake, through our commute to work, we are putting on armor. We assume protective body language, facial expressions, and attitudes. We close our heart. We are preparing for war and the daily assaults we are used to. We may have started the morning in bed, yawning and purring like kittens. But by the time we step into the building we are piranhas, poised for attack and to be attacked. The armor we wear at work determines our daily experiences. Hard, closed surfaces, like armor, can bruise and hurt colleagues and clients. They respond to us mutually, putting on their armor.

Someone needs to be the first to take off all this armor. Let yourself soften. Examine the benefits of losing your battlefield habits and acquiring habits for peace and relationship. Remind yourself of these benefits when you feel like putting your armor back on. Your tone, touch, words, actions, and energy can all be armor. They can also be gestures that say, *I care about you, and I am a safe place to be*. Watch yourself become a peacemaker. Notice how beauty gravitates to you, and your day grows easier. Practice this on your own, and together. You may feel vulnerable at first. Eventually you will realize that you were most vulnerable when you moved through work like a knight in shady armor.

BE EASY ON YOURSELF

Are you hard on yourself? How much time have you spent examining the roots of this behavior? For many, likely not enough. An unwell social environment grows very uncomfortable when you examine your own truth. And if you are hard on yourself, friend, this behavior has roots. Were you yelled and screamed at as a child? Raged at? Beaten? Criticized, doubted, guilt-tripped, ignored? If so, this may be the root of you being hard on yourself.

First, someone was hard on you. You figured they knew what they were doing, so you imitated.

Once you recognize this, you can go about transforming it. Let's say your objective is to learn how to be easy on yourself. Along the way, you will need to learn not to feel guilty about being easy on yourself. Through repeated ripples of gentleness in the way you touch your interior, being kind and tender comes to feel natural. One day, you pause and see how self-Loving you are, and how good it feels. Like freedom and safety. You realize being hard was never a life requirement. Now you are a presence of ease in the world who touches everything lightly. You are medicine. An endless springtime of beauty.

PATIENCE IS A VIRTUE

Many work cultures keep alive a story that they suffer from too little time. In reality, they may suffer more from too little patience. Patience is a fascinating phenomenon. It starts in the mind, filters through the body, and emerges as a self-fulfilling prophecy. When we practice patience, time magically becomes forgiving. When we practice impatience, we could have five hours and it would still feel like five minutes. Impatience is a choice to be stressed and anxious. It is a determination not to breathe, to tense up, and to spread our anxious energy to others. Patience is a blessing we offer. A mist of calm that spreads through the workplace valley. Patience, then, empowers our best self and purest giftedness. It is a reverberating example. A wonderful contagion. Patience is the act of providing space for things to happen. Rather than shrinking the walls and ceiling of a moment, we hold those perceptual foundations in place, having faith that if we just keep the moment going, good things will occur.

Patience is resented and renounced in an unwell environment, but celebrated in a tribe on a healing path. Patient cultures feel safe to children and families in need, and to the workers and leaders who require just as much patience. Patience is an internal exercise, a group agreement, a tribal fruit. Patience is what we preach to system-involved parents and adults. And a sermon of which we too might take heed.

GOSSIP

Gossip is a form of flatulence to which many people have grown so accustomed, they don't know what pleasant fragrance smells like and don't appreciate being around it. Let's stop gossip-bombing each other. Here is a practice tool: When invited into gossip, and we always are, simply remain quiet. Silence douses gossip, which always wants a partner. We fear personal and group rejection, so gossip is hard to resist. Try thinking of it as poison. Remind yourself that you'd rather not drink poison. And when you find yourself in a spew of gossip, know that you have the power to clear the air.

You can also start a trend for a whole new kind of gossip. Make your new-school gossip honest and adulating. Spread verifiable rumors about people's kindness, grace, humility, patience, heart, and inner beauty. Drop your Love gossip (gospel) like essential oils in the social spaces you feel need to be refreshed. Burn it like incense where negativity is fouling the room. Use it as an open window to let fresh air revitalize this place of servitude where you all spend so much time.

REMEMBER TO FORGET

Healing is in part an act of forgetting. Not absolute forgetting, but moving certain thoughts and their attendant feelings to the perimeter of our daily attention. Do this thoroughly and we minimize the influence of hurt on our habitual being. Our being is not an object, not a hard thing. It is a fluidity, a result of habit. So we are training our being to hold certain thoughts at the center, and other thoughts at the margins. We are not neglecting or ignoring our hard stuff, we are assigning it to its proper place: manageable spaces that allow us to breathe and function. Forgetting becomes a way for us to practice not obsessing, not being consumed, not being lost in our trauma, fear, and negativity. We forget, then, as a practice tool, a foundation for optimism and the kind of energy others want to be around.

FORGET TO REMEMBER

Another way to look at this is that sometimes we spend too much time remembering something painful. This imbalance creates a rupture in our relationship with our true self. We perceive that we *are* our pain, mistaking the amount of time we spend with our pain as evidence that we must *be* our pain. Our counter, then, is to practice not remembering. We learn to forget to remember our pain. We don't have to be afraid of losing our pain. This is not possible. We are not betraying it. We are caring for it by letting it rest in a space of ordinate, balanced attention. We visit it in mindful moments to nurture it into further dissolution.

A common belief: *The more time we spend remembering our pain, the more we are healing it.* Personally and as groups, we can practice another belief and see what it yields: *The more time we spend forgetting to remember our pain, the more space we create for remembering our joy, beauty, and possibility.* Everything needs space to grow. How about a system culture that intrinsically creates attentional gardens of wellness?

NO FLY ZONE

Establish a *No Fly Zone*. Maybe your office, cubicle, or workspace. Or your favorite chair in the lunchroom. Even a spot in the hallway or outside by a tree. Maybe your zone is your own body: Wherever you are, there is your zone.

Make your rules for this zone known to your people: "This is my No Fly Zone. When I am here, no drama allowed. No negativity, panic, stress, or anything that disturbs my peace. My peace is priceless to me." Ideally, you will grow so quiet in your zone that you hear nothing but the sound of your own breath, like a breeze through a valley. You are so still you can feel your heartbeat, a drum calling you home.

The point of your No Fly Zone is not to escape your work, but to prepare you for it. You go to your zone to recover, reflect... to regain your composure, center, and balance. Your zone also becomes an example to others that maybe they should get their own zone, instead of trying to get in on yours. You can have group zones, but this one, this one right here, is yours. Inspire a legion of zones. Oases of Peace, one for each staff person in a broad expanse of daily challenges.

It is important that we shape the expectations others have of how they can treat us. People try to get away with what they feel you will allow. Your zone is a radiance that leaves them saying to themselves: *Don't mess with her when she's in her zone. In fact, don't mess with her at all. She's not that kind. She's the kind who cares about how she is treated and how she treats herself. Let me fly my drama flag elsewhere.*

REVIVE YOUR FLOWER

When we notice a flower dying, we see the part of the flower above ground. Blossom, leaves, stem. But the dying is really happening below ground, in the roots. It started there. To understand what is happening to the flower, we need to understand what is happening to the roots.

To understand your suffering in relation to your work, it is not enough to focus on what is happening to you above ground. Your attitudes and behavior on the job, these are the easily visible parts of your suffering, of your unwellness. The roots of who you are in your work have to do with your calling. Your purpose and passion. Your nature as a child that led you to care about children, families, and those in crisis and need. These are your roots. Purpose and calling cannot be damaged. Your relationship with them can. If you are struggling with how you feel about your work, or about yourself in your work, it may be that you have become disconnected from your true purpose roots.

Can you rediscover and revitalize your purpose while remaining in this same job or work? This is a key question. When we are feeling down and beat up, our answer might be prejudiced. It might be more productive to say: *Let me start by seeing if I can find my purpose again, here where I am. If I can unearth it, great. If not, I will address that when I come to it.* To find your purpose, to engorge your tether to your passion, it helps to spend time talking and thinking about who you are. Who you began life as. What you used to dream about, yearn for, and tell yourself you were going to do with your life. Can you remember those tender moments so many years ago? They are still with you, in your heart.

Life has a way of pulling us away from the shore of our true nature, if we are not careful. Stress, pain, imbalance, illusions, and chosen priorities act like a riptide in the ocean. We wander too far out into the water and are swept away by these powerful forces. Tumbling underwater, we finally surface only to see that we cannot see. Our shore. Our true nature. If we stay out there in foreign waters too long, we can begin to forget our true nature. This makes the way home very difficult.

To keep sight of our shore, to swim back, we have to stay in touch with our true nature. We need to make it our central conversation again. A conversation within. Journaling and even mumbling to yourself can help. Share with others. Ask others to share with you their purpose and passion. This is good for bonding and can inspire your passions to stir and awaken. Invest in an honest examination of your work and make real effort to find connections between aspects of your work and aspects of your nature and calling. This takes time and patience. It is not a one-time exercise.

As you begin to see what your passion roots are missing, what they need to be fed, and what needs to be removed from their presence, take action. You are the only protector of your roots. No one else can do this for you. Advocate at work for those changes that you feel will help you and your colleagues or staff to renew their purpose. Become enthusiastic about caring for your roots. Create the conditions in your life and work for your roots to become well again. As this happens, your flower will regain its luster and vitality. Then something magical happens: Our social nature causes us to go from flower to flower, pollinating. Your entire workplace becomes a field of bright and fragrant flowers aglow with purpose.

LEAD YOURSELF TO WATER

When people lead us to water, we are grateful. Thing is, what do we do if they are not around? We start panicking, confusing the idea that we can't find water with the idea that there is no water. In this work, are we telling ourselves that there is no water (support, positivity, time, resources, validation, etc.)? If so, why? Because we want someone to lead us to water and we believe no one is leading? Or is it because we have no faith in our ability to find our own water?

Some of us are good at using the obvious water that is easily available in our daily work. But we may not have developed the muscle for finding the hidden water. The blessings that exist deeper down, that we have to dig for. Rather than develop that digging muscle, we choose helplessness. We freeze. We bring every challenge to someone else to take care of. We tell ourselves, *I don't have training for this*. We find the exit sign and check out of the exit door.

Creativity is not something you put on a program calendar and then it mystically appears. Creativity is a spirit. One that needs to be encouraged and cultivated in people and workplaces. If you have to bring in a group of children to help the adults give themselves permission to be creative, go ahead and arrange for the busloads. Actually, I was joking, but that might not be a bad idea.

We can lead ourselves to water. This is a practice tool. Emphasis on *practice*. The thing about water (resources and blessings) is that it wants to be found. It emits an energy that is like a bird calling out for a mate. In your work, your need and initiative form that mate. If you dare to look for water, you are more than halfway to finding it. It will sense your endeavor and leap up through the sand, percolating obviously on the surface before you. This is how creativity and problem solving work. Those dynamics don't respond to us being closed, helpless, and frozen. They jump into our arms the moment we open, act, warm, and help ourselves.

Whatever we need, we can lead ourselves to water. As we do, others are inspired to do the same. Workers inspire leaders. Leaders inspire workers. Everyone becomes a leader. Water is suddenly everywhere. The whole tribe drinks.

OUR CREATIVITY ORGAN

Every organ in our body needs to be cared for. This includes our creativity organ, which is not physiological as much as it is holistic. It involves our whole being. To take care of our creative organ, we need to flush it through with creativity. You keep your heart healthy by making sure that blood is flushing through it cleanly.

Same with our creativity organ. It was designed to be a vessel filled with flow of expansion, growth, discovery, building, and transformation. Stay in this stream with your work, and you keep your creativity organ strong. In return, it serves you when you really need it. Some believe they lack this organ. No such person exists. We wouldn't make it through even the first year of life. What we might perceive as an absent creativity organ is instead an atrophied one. The great thing is, this atrophy can be quickly reversed. Don't imagine your work as a tedious chore, a repetitive conveyor belt of procedures. See it as an art project, a blank canvas, an empty gallery. Live each day with creative abandon. Spill the paint of your personality all over the place.

FIND YOUR SACRED LAKE

Animals, when weary or wounded, go to the places they know will be safe. They go there for respite and to lick their wounds. They rest, reflect, renew. In many places around the world, people have sacred places in their cultures where they go for rest and renewal. Nature offers many of these sacred places. In Nepal, I learned of and visited several sacred lakes. Local people consider these bodies of water sacred for their spiritual history and energy they hold and exude. And for their healing qualities, and the reverence they demand.

When serving human lives, we all have a great need for sacred lakes. Places within our workday we can visit for rest, reflection, and renewal. These aren't always physical spaces. They can be thought spaces. Feeling spaces. Ceremonies, traditions, and habits, however small or quirky. We need our personal sacred lakes. Teams and units need their sacred lakes. Organizations and programs (tribes) need their sacred lakes.

Ideally, our personal lakes are places of solitude and quietude. *Solitude...* Not the absence of others, but the presence of ourselves with ourselves. *Quietude...* Not silence, but the sound and sermon of our own soul. We grow lonely for ourselves during the day and don't even realize it. The desire to be alone is not in conflict with our work. It is a sign that we need to refill our tank with vitality water only solitude and quietude offer. Organizations have no reason to leave their workforces dehydrated in this way, out of a misguided conviction that we must never pause to tend to ourselves. That we must always work, work, work, even until the loss of health or life. Solitude and quietude are not truancy from work. They are wells from which our work water is drawn.

Our sacred places must be preserved, kept pure, not desecrated. We can make agreements that we will not pollute these spaces with our drama or negativity. Drama being the chosen and harmful expression of our valid hurt or grievance. We agree that our sacred lakes will be respected by all, that we will collectively grant permission to each other to visit our sacred lakes as needed, that we will not treat these visits as superfluous, or a distraction from the work. We agree that our time in our various sacred lakes *is* the work. It is our preparation for the work. Our reflective development of the work. Our assurance of fruitfulness in the work.

We agree that whatever our titles or roles, we will honor the centrality of our sacred lakes in keeping everyone well and enabling us to help the community be well. Our sacred lakes will not exist at the margin of our day but will be situated within our flow. We will not have to go trekking to that water during rare breaks, rushed lunches, or only after the work is done and we are heading home. It will be our ever-available space and spirit of *caring* for we who do this work. Do this, and we may witness the spectacular assumption of peace and vibrancy within our climate. We may even begin to act, think, feel, and dream sacredly.

WASH YOUR DAY OFF

Your personal life outside of work can be your greatest sacred lake. Each moment away from work is an opportunity to wash off the sediment of the day, and flush out your trauma-laden thoughts, feelings, and tension. Do what cleanses and heals you. This is not necessarily the same as what numbs you. Numbing stimulus can be tempting, though it does not necessarily repair us from our workday or renew us for the next one. When you are not at work, exist as though you are on vacation from work. Shed worries and the visualizing of mental tasks. Treat yourself to what feeds you. Time in nature, quietude, solitude, socializing. Write poetry, read books, take long walks. Restore that old truck or antique furniture.

Lose yourself in your Loved ones. The idea is to empty your cup of whatever sediment work fills you with, so you have room and rest to be filled again by the work journey ahead. Always be emptying sediment and filling with peace. Find your true vibration and the two of you spend the whole night together.

GRATITUDE AND GRACE

A positive attitude does not depend on life or work conditions in order to exist. And in existing, it creates the most beautiful conditions. One great seed we can plant for a positive attitude is gratitude. Not just thankfulness, but continuous testimony in the heart chamber to the miracle and Grace of being alive, and of our servitude. Think about it: As children we dreamed of helping to save the world. Now we are doing it. Somehow, someone gave us the awesome privilege of being at the center of people's struggles. To have a hand in the changing of their condition. You are a professional world changer. Is this not something to cherish? You get to touch these particular lives in your particular way. Those lives will carry your imprint, sometimes forward over generations. You will carry their imprint. You will be deepened. Grooved. Polished and clarified. Washed in their tears.

Today, choose one thing for which you are grateful. Celebrate that one thing all day long. For, in the midst of true cherishing, it is difficult to be dreary or pessimistic. Don't make room for what thieves your Light. Just keep singing *Grateful* in your brightest voice.

Tomorrow, choose another thing for which to be grateful, and celebrate just as persistently. Soon, you will be a living habit of gratitude, and your spirit's composure will tend toward joyfulness. The conditions of your work, being greatly impressionable, will follow.

When your gratitude grows larger than your worries, you are on your way to peace. What matters is that we tend the right garden. This takes discipline, focus, and being present with ourselves so that we can resist the distractions and illusions that work brings.

Gratitude dilates the heart, and lets the soul sense its kinship with all things. In this state of kinship, our work relationships shimmer with an energy of alliance, a sense that we are all in this together, whether or not we wish it; therefore, we should care for each other.

Much of what we are wrestling with is ego. Ours. That of others. Ego is a hot air balloon, constantly wanting to rise and be seen. Humility is the thousand daily arrows of Grace and Gratitude that gently bring it down. Staying humble in an egoistic world and vocation is hard work. It requires the daily dissolving of our self-ideas into an idea of our larger, dissipated self. Our collective, tribal self. As we grow accustomed to experiencing life outside of our individual concerns, we carve out a space in the heart for gratitude. A sense that all that is good in our life and work is not to be taken for granted. That it can disappear tomorrow. That we could easily be the next one in need of crisis care or system services. In our work, we can choose between two deciding practices: the daily listing of laments or the collecting of gratitude. Both have predictable outcomes. You know which path to take.

THE POWER OF THE PERSON

One person can change the group. This is a fundamental social psychological truth. We believe in this truth when it comes to negative impact. We have seen too many times how one person can change the very air of a staff meeting or training by exuding negativity or anger. But our faith in *the power of one* seems shaken when we are asked to be a part of positive group change. To help with your faith, survey your life. Can you recall times when a stranger's smile made you feel good inside? When someone's single word or comment soothed your hurting heart? Or when a kind encouragement helped you with a bout with fear and doubt? Your life reveals the truth. Always seek out your own story for the evidence you need.

If things are going to improve at work, we each need to strengthen our faith in the power of the single person. Pay attention around the workplace to instances of positive singular influence. Not just the obvious single persons, such as a director or manager. Notice how the warm energy and expressions of administrative support, security, facilities management, or IT staff affect the environment. Pay attention to those who are usually unseen and disregarded. Celebrate and engage with them. Take note of how their kindness makes you feel, and of how your kindness makes them feel. We fail to practice mutual care and kindness largely because we are suffering crises of faith. If we spend more time seeing the truth of positive personal power, this witnessing can renew our faith and restore our sense of self-determination.

COMPASSION OF SKY

Nature is one of the best guides for how we can exist in our work. Take the sky, for example. It is a master practitioner of lightness. It does not anxiously hold onto clouds, wind, and water. It lets them do what they do and keep on moving. The sky always stays more composed than the disturbances that move through it. Sky realizes its true nature is larger than any disturbance. It never panics, never acts as though it, the sky, is falling. We can practice the compassion and lightness of the sky. Letting what happens in our day, with people, pass through gently, have its moment, serve its purpose. Then, we can release and let go. Letting go of our emotions is hard for us. And yet, what is the purpose of our emotions? Do they come so that we can lose ourselves in them? Or are they here for us to use, allowing them to do what they do, and pass on? We forget that we are not our emotions, not the difficult moments. We are larger than those things. We existed before them and will after them. We are the sky. Remembering this, we bless our work.

COMPASSION OF FLOWERS

Sometimes it feels as though we are little more than a pincushion, a helpless place where external forces come and dump on us. Not a good feeling. But what might appear to be a passive recipient can actually be a very active participant. Take flowers. We see bees, butterflies, and birds coming and going, landing, poking, prodding, perching. These animals seem to have their way with flowers, getting what they want of nectar and seeds. If we look deeper we see that flowers allow all of this to happen. Flowers allow this interplay to occur by choosing to open and remain open. Flowers know that this circle of life, and its purpose, are fulfilled only with the flowers' cooperation. Flowers understand that they benefit from the pollination that occurs.

It is the flower that is practicing the power of the person. In this case, the flower person allows various forces and relationships to interact with it, knowing that ultimately this dynamic, this give and take, this mutual, symbiotic dance will leave the flower more able to be a healthy flower, and to serve in the birthing and flourishing of more new flowers. Serving lives is a craft of pollination. Of doing what it takes and allowing what is required to create communities and climates of healthy flowers. Too flowery? Just put it this way: If you are open, relationship both delivers and spreads good things that make you feel good and others feel good. Good enough?

UNCONDITIONAL COMPASSION

Let's be real. Don't we sometimes practice conditional compassion? Do you ever find yourself considering different coworkers or service recipients, deciding whether they deserve your compassion? Our internal conversation can be absurd: *She doesn't deserve my compassion because she just got promoted and I didn't. I'm not going to give him any warmth because he's my superior. None for that person in need because he's too far beneath my social status. That person dresses too shabbily. That person is a little too crazy. That woman isn't in my unit. That man works in a different branch. She's too thin. He's too muscular. I don't know her well enough. That's a teen with a bad attitude, so, no. I would be kind to her, but she gave me a thoughtless gift seven years ago at the holiday party.*

We go on like this, secretly determining whether to hand out compassion as though it's our private stash of premium candy. But compassion is not ours. It lives in us only so that it may flow from us. When we fail to practice this, we suffer more than anyone we keep from our compassion. When we hoard compassion, it grows rancid in us, becomes something else. Something acidic. Warmth withheld bruises the compassion organ, diluting and polluting your warmth even for those you like. Your warmth for yourself is also diminished. So go ahead, give people some of your sugar. The world around you will be a whole lot sweeter.

WORK JOYFULLY

The spirit in which we work matters. Working grimly is self-fulfilling: We experience work as grim. Our prism is a cataract of gloom. All we see is sullen and heavy. Working joyfully is also self-fulfilling. This spirit casts a brightness and lightness over everything. Even a dull and uninspiring place of work. Working joyfully is like splashing sunlight on all your paperwork, coworkers, and service relationships. No one shivering says, "Less sunlight please." People are cold and could use a hug. Be a hugging tree. Watch as others appear, in apparently random ways, to be in your presence. Their approach is never random.

Your joy is a gravity. A medicine. A balm for tenderness. It costs you no time, money, or resources. In fact, working joyfully can enrich your time, money, and resources. It is a fountain from which community and system drink and cool themselves. The result is not just better outcomes, but also a new spirit in the tribe and land. One of abundance, which manifests in all the ways we can dream of, and more. Practicing joy is like splurging on oxytocin and dopamine, the stress relieving, calming chemicals that kindly subdue inflammatory adrenaline and cortisol within us. It's like a tropical vacation in the heart, sipping beachside on an umbrella drink. We could have worse things to practice.

EASY ENTITLEMENTS

In this human work of ours, we seem to entitle ourselves to all the wrong things. Subconsciously and otherwise, we entitle ourselves to fatigue, negativity, resentment, fear, and insecurity. These are easy entitlements, even though their energy feels bad to us. This is because we can simply fall into them. But healthful entitlements are also well within our reach: hopefulness, optimism, deep compassion, freedom, initiative, patience. Healthful entitlements take work, require us to break the adhesion of old, deep habits. Yet these entitlements feel so very good, unleash so much fruitfulness.

When it comes to feeling good in your work, practice entitling yourself.

REDEFINE YOUR WORK

When you think about your work, do the thoughts produce unpleasant feelings? If so, it is likely that the way you define your work could use a tune-up. This does not mean that the difficult aspects of your vocation are invalid, or that how they make you feel is invalid. But there is an opportunity here to nestle what is unpleasant inside of a larger meaning and purpose that feels pleasant.

Start with the ordering of your thoughts. If your first thoughts about work tend to be about people and things you don't like, you are defining your work according to distaste and not purpose. Your passion and calling should always be the first wave of thoughts. That wave can then cradle the difficult thoughts and feelings that come after, dilute them into a milder energy. As you practice placing purpose first in your work definition, the definition itself begins to change. It takes on a meaning that serves you and your inner peace, rather than serving any chaos and dysfunction that exist in your environment.

Serve yourself. Define your work according to the essence in it that attracted you in the first place. Highlight the parts that move and fulfill you. The pieces and people you cherish. The precious opportunities. Bring joy out of your work definition closet, out into the living room of your conscious mind and heart. Positive definitions need to be practiced, or they become run over by negative narratives inherited by pollution in your social climate. This kind of practice keeps positivity and purpose at the surface of your being, saturates you in the elements that keep you warm and whole.

MIND YOUR IMPRINT

Every person in your tribe is continuously affecting every other person. Hope that you are positively affecting, and not infecting. You leave a lasting imprint through each aspect of your being. We underestimate this imprint, so we are careless with it. Think of littering. The more people are made conscious of their responsibility not to litter, and the more they see how they literally pollute the world, the less likely they are to litter. But littering was not always in the cultural consciousness. It had to be introduced. A story began and was spread. Laws and policies were created. Consequences administered. Over years, the idea of not littering became something people thought about. And even so, we still find plenty of people littering, especially when they feel they can get away with it.

When we are at work, our *way of being* is a form of teaching, of influencing. A prime social example. Negative role modeling happens all the time. There is no such thing as neutrality in our role modeling. We are role modeling something helpful, or something harmful, but we are always role modeling. Choose wisely. Unleash the power and radiance of your smile. This will flush you and others with feel-good hormones, and set a great example. Handle your moments with grace and character because your people are watching. Kindness, compassion, and positivity can be codified and measured by agencies in a way that creates standards and expectations. The nation of Bhutan has achieved this with their *Gross National Happiness Index* and related cultural initiative. If an entire society can go on such a journey, we need to stop believing that our systems are too large or seriously minded for the same kind of transformation.

Now is our time to develop system cultures in which people don't feel they can get away with leaving a harmful imprint. I'm not suggesting a punitive approach, but rather a corrective one. Not a climate of shaming, but an atmosphere of accountability: Inner pride in not energetically and behaviorally littering the workplace. Social celebration of those who are good at leaving a clean and healthy imprint. Every movement needs effective public (organizational) announcements. Rallying cries and campaigns. Have fun with it. Be creative about creating a cultural consciousness in each worker and leader. Most of us know this phrase about caretaking our great outdoors: *Leave it like you found it.* Develop a culture in your workplace that says, loud and clear, to those who come and those who stay: *In our tribe, we take care of our imprint.*

WORD POWER

You are what you eat. Also, you are what you speak. Use the word *Love* a lot. And mean it. The more you evoke it, the more you become it. Like yoga of the mouth and soul. You are opening, stretching yourself into the caring vessel you were born as. Breaking old adhesions of closure and obstruction. We shouldn't have to remind each other to say 'thank you' for everything. Let's remind each other anyway. Say 'thank you,' *for everything*. Speak caring. Speak kindness. Speak purpose and passion. Whatever you do not speak, you do not become. Don't let harmful words become your daily practice or mode for managing stress. You will not be managing stress. You will be inviting it. So pick up this amazing instrument called language. Become known for beautiful music. Examine the language you are using with each other. There you will discover where you are healthy and where you are ailing. Language is a great litmus test. Staff meetings are a convenient place to examine language, not combatively, but supportively. Say, "We are going on a language journey together. How are we doing with our word?"

TONE POWER

Tone of voice matters greatly. With the right tone, we can convey sincerity and compassion, diffuse conflict, and touch trauma in a way that is healing. Whether over the phone, in writing, or in person, our tone at the point of first contact with a colleague or client has tremendous impact. It can be a welcome offering all by itself. Learn to be in tune with your tone, especially under duress. Use tone as a tool to be a social facilitator of wellness and healing. You are a born virtuoso of tone. It's just a matter of practice. Notice the tones of coworkers. Merge with the ones that feel good to you. Now you have harmony, music that makes the world go 'round.

PAY ATTENTION

Simply by slowing down, being present, and allowing our natural caring nature, sensitivity, and intuition to manifest, we can be more in touch with how our coworkers are doing, and how we ourselves are doing. Noticing is the first step in caring. Paying attention to ourselves and to each other is a tool that enriches our caring practice. Attention doesn't cost energy or time. It saves both by making us more efficient and effective as we proceed. So much gets missed when we fail to pay attention. But when we tune in, we turn on our greatness.

KINDNESS

People come up with all kinds of wild reasons why they cannot afford to be kind. For your work culture to be a kind one, you depend on a critical mass of people who are devoted to being kind, and to countering the false tribal stories about why kindness cannot be afforded. Kindness does not take time. It saves time by strengthening work relationships, and improving the health and wellness of workers and leaders. Thus, work is done more efficiently. Kindness and correction can exist in the same breath. The idea that correction must be harsh and unkind is a myth in many workplace tribes. Correction is an act of discipline rooted in a caring spirit. We correct people because we want and need better for them and from them. This motive can be communicated kindly.

With stress, kindness is the first thing to go. We shrink into ourselves, erecting shields against the world, even against our most Loved ones. To protect kindness in our work, we need to manage and eradicate stress. Kindness is an all-around winner. It makes people feel safer at work, and deepens people's sense of belonging. Kindness dissolves stress, soothes emotional wounds, and makes people want to show up and be fully present. Kindness is a tranquilizer, sedative, and antidote to anxiety and crisis. Not a bad prescription. And keep in mind: People who look for excuses not to be kind are simply determined to be unkind. The great thing is that kindness is a determination, too. Remember, those around you are thirsty. Through your warmth, offer them regular sips of grace. Kindness is a form of poetry. Write a thousand daily verses.

GENTLY

Do you know why flowers don't mind butterflies? Because butterflies land on flowers gently. *A butterfly lands on a thousand flowers, never leaving a single bruise.* We might learn from this. Without care, we bruise and hurt each other regularly, without intent or awareness. People react to this harm by being hard and harsh back to us. We wonder why people are treating us so poorly, not realizing that we are participating in a culture of social battering. Gentleness is good practice. It allows work processes a smoother riverbed through which to flow. Be a practitioner of gentle touch, of butterfly nature in your various ways: Word. Gaze. Listening. Movement. Choices. Memories. Be the light breeze in your valley that soothes all the trees (people) and leaves them smiling.

CULTIVATE LIKING

Let's say you dislike someone at work. What do you do with this dislike? Allow it to ferment, as though you plan to bottle it like wine and sell it at the office? You may have many takers, but you'll poison the workplace and your work. You could invest emotionally in changing the person you dislike, but if they don't change, you'll resent them in addition to disliking them. One option you can control: Spend time with your feelings of dislike. Explore why the person affects you in such a way. Apply Loving attention to this sore spot in you. Gradually ease the dislike into a feeling of honest recognition. Have compassion for yourself and the other person regarding your true feelings. Talk to your dislike. Soothe and assure it, as you would a baby. Dislike actually is a baby in us, or rather, the baby we were. It scrunches up its face and says, "I don't like that." Being a baby, though, dislike isn't content to simply express dislike. It feels it must also pitch a fit. This happens at work in interesting ways: You treat the person with avoidance, resistance, meanness, closure, attack. So, soothe your inner baby. Promise it that you won't let it get hurt. Fear of getting hurt is what dislike, in a primal way, is all about.

Reflect on the fact that you don't actually know the person well, so it is really your idea of the person that you dislike. What their appearance, voice, behavior, and attitudes feel like to you. The whole person? You don't know that being, not entirely. In moments of conflict, remind yourself: *I do not know her (his) story at all.* Remind yourself of how little others know of your own story, even family and friends, much less coworkers. Do not assume the motives of others. This is how groups grow hostile within. Instead, transfer your presumption of your own good intentions into your projection of other people's intent. Develop a habit of imagining good intention.

Your experience of disliking is a wrestling match with an idea of someone. This presents an opportunity. You can just as easily imagine attractive elements of the person and his or her life as you have been imagining unattractive qualities. So, practice. Exercise empathy and compassion for all the qualities you imagine. You can also make an effort to get to know the person better. This intent and the energy it carries might change the person's way of being with you. Wanting to know someone is a powerful compliment to them, a dose of caring for their insecurity and sense of belonging. What you discover in them may include both appealing and unappealing truths. But at least you will have broader, deeper perspective, from which compassion tends to flow. Inspire a group culture where people see each other's true hearts beyond misleading surface impressions. Become *heart seers.*

Remember, your dislike creates the most harmful burden inside of you. You are the one who has to carry it around all day, every day. It ferments and expands until you become a heavy wine cellar stocked full with bitter vintages of dislike. This can be your choice. Or, you can go about breaking all the bottles, letting the bitterness evaporate. Do this, and you'll have nothing left to offer your colleagues for their thirst except your harvested lightness of being.

POSITIVITY IS A RADIATION TREATMENT

Radiation is always being emitted in your workplace and out in the field. Sunlight. False light. And human energy. It's the human stuff you need to look out for. The good news is that you can control what you are radiating. When you choose positivity, your radiation can travel right to the seed of another person's suffering and become a part of their healing. Or, your radiation can simply lighten people's mood, or calm their anxiety. As with any radiation treatment, precise targeting matters. Target your positivity beam where you feel it is needed most. Treat the sore spots. General exposure is great, too, so canvass the whole area. Just make sure you turn the beam inward, and treat yourself as needed. And, as always, tell this story of your radiation. Let your people know about this old technology, and how well it is working for you.

GIVE GOOD FACE

Our face is full of numerous muscles, each capable of telling a story to others, through obvious expressions, and through micro expressions. As adults, there is no reason for us not to use our face responsibly. We underestimate its influence on others, which leads us to be careless about what stories it transmits. In the high stress environment of our work, our face can be a tremendous calming instrument, for ourselves and others. Even if we don't see our face, how we choose to express it creates an inner response. For others, subconsciously and consciously, they are reacting to our face. Imitating it. Like a child looking to its parent for cues as to how to feel in a particular moment or situation. Or, they are being triggered into good or bad feelings by our facial canvas. Check your face. Ask yourself: *Why am I frowning? Can I choose another face?*

Some leaders and workers are very good at setting tone through their expression. Without even saying a word, they influence the collective mood. Others move through their day with little face consciousness, spilling their every inner conflict onto colleagues or clients with each pinch or pursing of their face. Give good face. It costs you nothing, takes no time, and gives you a lasting facial. It also provides a rejuvenated measure of influence over the atmosphere. *Face* your space.

ZEN YOUR FLOW

Our nervous system follows our body's lead. Walk calmly, and the nervous system takes this to mean you are calm, then acts accordingly. Be mindful of how you are moving. Drink and eat in calm motions. Like a tea ceremony. Pay attention to the sensations that come with the act. Your fingers on the cup. The warmth that spreads. The steam that mists your face. The feeling of liquid on your lips. The heat flowing into your mouth and down your throat. Get lost in that and you may even lose track of what you were just worrying about the moment before.

Use your body as a graceful instrument, always sending yourself calming signals. When you turn your head, do so slowly. Stand up and sit down calmly. All day long, use your body to persuade your mind and nerves that you are not in a rush, not a hot mess of nerves, but that you are the embodiment of tranquility. Sometimes you have to fool yourself until you become the inner state you desire.

BE A CHEETAH

Please bear with me as I veer again into the animal kingdom. People imagine that cheetahs are always sprinting. I imagine cheetahs are insulted by this stereotype. Perhaps they are even forming a crowdfunded awareness campaign as we speak. The reality is that cheetahs spend most of their time resting and recovering from sprinting. They spend a great deal of time contemplating life. This makes them wise sprinters. Cheetahs spend as much time resting and reflecting as tortoises, who have also been misrepresented. Tortoises are not lazy. They just do a lot of visualization. Before each and every step. What appears to us to be slow motion movement is the tortoise enjoying the moment within each step.

We can learn from cheetahs and tortoises. Just because we are required to sprint through a certain work task, does not mean that we have to keep on sprinting, all day long. We are most efficient, effective, and healthy, when we learn when to sprint and when not to sprint. As soon as a sprint-task is done, it is okay not to sprint through your next breath. Ask yourself: *Why am I sprinting through chewing my food? Drinking my coffee? Why am I sprinting through my thoughts? Sprinting through my bathroom break, sprinting out to the car after work?* Be a cheetah. Stop sprinting when you don't have to. Rest is good. Recovery is great. Reflection helps you not to have to sprint so much the next time.

Be a tortoise. Visualize optimum movement through each and every moment. Cherish each moment as a delicacy even if it tastes like utter garbage. Create your own private desserts sprinkled with peace.

A MORNING MEDITATION

This morning, as you stretch your waking body, hopefully you will stretch your waking spirit. Wash it clean in a basin of purification. Say to yourself: "Today I will speak only sacred words... in my mind, throughout my heart, and across my lips. Today I will reject the seduction of anger, ugliness, prejudice, and judgment. I will devote my life in this place between sunrise and moonrise to practicing new habits that lift me to new altitudes of Beauty and Lovingness. I will mend my heart with a thread and needle of meditation upon *compassion*. I will remember why I am here in the world, to be Love... and I will forget the hurtfulness that this world encourages me to be. I will walk the ground of this day with light and Loving footsteps upon Earth, planting seeds of Hope everywhere I go."

SEE MIRACLES

Everything in our work is a miracle. Every single part of our work could easily go horribly wrong in an instant. Yet, each day, most things do not go wrong. They work out. This is miraculous. If we practice seeing our work reality as a miracle, our whole being changes. What we resonate grows more positive and hopeful, which in turn transforms our environment, relationships, and processes. Miracles are wonderfully found where we look for them.

INTIMACY

We are taught during our professional journey that intimacy with those we serve is not a good thing. Examine this idea. You might discover that in many ways this is a work tribe myth. Intimacy is that quality of a relationship that involves sharing. How is it then that you can share resources and services without being intimate?

This seems contradictory. Further, if you are practicing the opposite of intimacy in your service provision, then you are practicing the same thing in your work relationships. What we practice with one person we practice with all people, whether we recognize it or not. Practice does not segregate. Our brain and nervous system only know that we are practicing a thing, so those systems become better at that thing. With intimacy, we are either getting better at it, or worse at it. There is no such thing as being in neutral. Think about how social intimacy plays a role in your personal relationships. Whatever you come up with, that is the role that social intimacy can also play in your work. We ask those we serve to open up and trust us. That's a lot of intimacy we expect from someone who doesn't know us. Maybe they could use a little reciprocation. Or a whole lot.

REMEMBER BEAUTY

Do you not remember the Love you have poured? The souls you have touched? Your compassion garden? Remember the precious moments of your work. Keep bringing them back, a fountain running through your soul. If you neglect these memories, you will become overrun and burdened by the difficult memories. They will distort your sense of self, like looking for your reflection in rippled or muddy water. Keep your water clear by remembering the purity of your heart and why you are here. Memory like this is a reflection pond. Go there to see yourself. To find yourself. Remember as medicine. As comfort and assurance. As hope and vision. For in your best memories, you find a window for seeing the abundant goodness still to come.

THE ART OF NOTICING BEAUTY

The more beauty you notice in your workday, the better you will feel and the more effectively you will work and serve. Notice the small things and feel your cherishing of them. Notice the efforts so many around you are making, despite the barriers they face. Notice the deeply soulful energy of people caring about each other. Notice the smiles, tears, hugs, and laughter. Notice the new plant on someone's desk, the motivational quote on someone's wall. Notice the beauty existing everywhere around you. Become a cultivator and a curator of those things. Fill your mind with your favorite flowers, and there will be little room for anything else, except the fragrance.

FLY YOUR FLAG

Representing our work, group, or agency to others on the outside is a psychological phenomenon that helps us fall in Love with the work all over. This is likely to happen with anything or anyone we represent in life. A primal part of us is triggered, an affiliation gene, if you will. When we claim something as part of who we are, this claiming ushers Love into our hearts. Place yourself and your colleagues in position to represent the work, especially to those who do not understand. Place people in position to represent the whole team or tribe. Just being in this position can change people's perspective and attitude about their work. The task forces them to more closely examine their work story and unearth its roots.

CURIOSITY

Curiosity is a trait possessed by inspired workers and leaders. A characteristic of passionate learners. Curiosity desires expansion and growth. It wants to sponge the world, to grow more intimate with it. Curiosity is not to be discouraged, which is what can happen in traumatized workplaces. Experiencing the discomfort of anxiety, we seek to alleviate the feeling by controlling others. Curiosity is a freedom that threatens our sense of control. If we examine together the roots of our need for control, we can see how destructive it is to our healing and helping work. The people we serve need our resourcefulness, not just our robotic delivery of resources. They need our creativity, vision, faith, hope, problem solving, and conflict resolving. All of these traits carry the persona of curiosity. Curiosity is a best practice for systems concerned with growth and transformation. Let's put it in the mix.

TEMPLE BELL

Thich Nhat Hanh shares a story about how he used to grow anxious when he was in a car in traffic and people started honking their horns. He was used to the serenity and quietude of the monastery. The harshness of traffic sounds and horns affected his inner peace. He longed for the familiar, calming sound of the temple bell in his monastery, a sound that called him into a deep, peaceful contemplation. Then, he had a realization: He could train his mind, heart, and body to associate the sound of car horns with the sound of his treasured temple bell. Since the brain is imminently cooperative, all it took was practice. When he heard a car blare its horn, he told himself that he was hearing the soothing song of the temple bell. It worked. When car horns shrieked, instead of growing anxious, his whole being envisioned and experienced the temple bell. He grew tranquil inside.

We have this same power, to change our stressful associations at work into more calming experiences. Make a list of all the small and large things in your workday that create stress and anxiety. Decide that you will not be so powerless anymore, that you will condition yourself to react to this stimuli in a way that serves your wellness. Turn your aggravating factors into your own tranquilizing temple bell.

ALL ABOUT THE GRAIN

Granular attention is important. Our rapidly moving society and culture condition us to notice the grandiose. But a sublime river is moving through and around us, and it is granular. Its details are as small as grains. If we look closer we see that in every grain there is a mountain. When we pay granular attention to positive examples and experiences in our work, we feed ourselves the nutrition that keeps us whole and complete. When we share those granular meanings with our leadership, who are often far away and disconnected from the granular social details of servitude, now we are teaching upward. We are empowering our leadership into a greater intimacy with workers and people served. Granularity is the fine art of creative people. It can yield spectacular results. It should be our fine art, too.

CHERISH THE WORK

What do you appreciate about your work? How often do you ask yourself this question? Stay in touch with both the question and your answers. It will help keep you in a place of gratitude, grace, and humility. From that space you can better manage the difficult aspects of work. Develop thought habits that run you through the feelings of cherishing your work. Keep going down to that river, wading into its waters, and soaking yourself in cherishment. It is a great tonic and way to anchor yourself in purpose and passion. When we actively cherish, feelings and chemicals are generated that wash us clean and remake our constitution for service.

TRUST

Trust is a high priority practice item. Work on trusting yourself. On trusting your staff, and your leadership. Though we are all adults, we too often show no more faith in each other to resolve issues than we do young children. Whether faced with a personal conflict or a work-related crisis, people have the ability to figure things out if they are left with no other choice. Frequently we don't provide others this opportunity. Our control impulse kicks in. We address the issue for them. This can be disempowering and disabling. We build trust by having faith, not by exercising doubt. And, of course, we develop trust through consistent attitude and action, relating to people in an honorable fashion over time until it becomes clear: The way we treat them is simply who we are.

STAYCATIONS

Make sure that during your day you are creating personal and team moments of relaxation, detachment, and peace. You say you don't have time for this? What about during those many moments when you aren't doing actual work, but instead are caught in a haze of worry or panic? You could use those brief seconds and minutes for a staycation. In fact, staycations are a great way for a workforce to maintain and nurture itself. Once staycations become habitual, everyone starts infecting everyone, over and over, with a creative fever. People eagerly look for and share new ways to relax for just a moment, to laugh together, to space out, to feel good inside.

SYSTEMS OF FEAR

What we like to call *systems of care* can often fairly be described as *systems of fear*. Because we have so neglected ourselves in the course of becoming modern, we are soaked in fear. This is what happens to neglected things. They grow fearful, insecure, wilted. We have beautiful souls doing this work. If we look closely, we see our fearful truth. Leaders are afraid to lead. Workers are afraid to work. Everyone is afraid to be honest and real with the people being served. We are afraid to believe in them, to inspire them, so we default to controlling them. Or at least attempting to. We attend conferences and pass around our fear. We provide and participate in trainings where we concentrate our fear. We conceive laws, policies, and practices loyal most of all to fear. Funding streams are shaped by fear. Fear of media attention, fear of social backlash, fear of letting go of a society that is not working. We are fixated on what we cannot do, should not do, better not do. Because we are so impressionable, we keep infecting each other with fear.

The only way out of this fear enterprise is to care for ourselves. Deeply. Together. Cared for things acquire composure, constitution, and fortitude. Cared for things are not as fearful. They are in the full flush of being their true nature, which doesn't leave time or priority for fearful contemplation. Our idea of being *modern* has been to conquer the world outside of ourselves. This is a cultural idea. Like all cultural ideas, it can be made extinct. Not all cultures are consumed in conquering. Some care about harmony and balance. This means we have examples. The possibility is proven. Creating actual systems of care is realistic. But the care aspect has to be alive within our professional realm. Within and between leaders, workers, and agencies. This will be a journey: learning to be caring. But caring nature is already in our human nature. We don't have to summon it from a lightning bolt in the sky. We need only stir it from beneath our modern sediment. It will be good to learn the language and ways of caring again. Then we may have something proper to consistently, culturally offer the people who need our care.

HARRIET TUBMAN

Harriet Tubman was a *baaad* woman. She didn't play. One story I appreciate telling about her (creatively adapted, of course) is a story of leadership. So, the story goes that Harriet and her people had been discussing for some time the idea of breaking away from their plantation and finding freedom. Now, freedom can be a very frightening idea to a slave. Sure enough, as the designated night approached in which the group would escape the plantation, the people began to voice their concerns. Their fears.

Many of these people were menfolk, and Harriet being a woman, was used to the challenges of being a female leader. Folks started in with fear talk: "Now, Harriet, this freedom thing of yours sounds great in theory, but I don't know if it is realistic. Look at our life. We have so much to deal with. So many bad things could go wrong. I don't know if we have time for this freedom thing. I need to get back to my work or *Massa gon' whup me good.* I can't afford to lose my job. How much work is this freedom thing going to require?"

Does this litany of fear talk sound familiar to you? If so, it is because, bless us all, the slave is alive and well in our society and work. It is a spirit of self-oppression that burrows deep into people and groups, rendering their idea of reality as one of impending doom.

Harriet listened respectfully to her people. But Harriet knew fear. It was in the nature of being a slave. In fact, her people harvested fear more than they harvested cotton or other crops. It was fear that they brought home to their slave quarters. Fear that they ate together for dinner. Beds of fear that they slept on. Dreams of fear in the night. Fear was their sunrise, their clothing, their daily industry. So, Harriet, she knew fear. And she would not let it get in the way of freedom. On a night absent of moonlight, Harriet gathered her people down by the riverbank. The murmuring water would be their chaplain for this freedom service. The people were now terrified. They risked death, dismemberment, whippings, dogs tearing at their flesh. They risked disappointing their overseers and their masters. They risked losing their precious jobs as house slaves, for few wanted the backbreaking life of a field slave. They risked being sold. This entire river of fears was now pushing up their throats, coming out as angry resistance to freedom.

Harriet wasn't sweet. She was fire. A woman, slave, nurse, social worker, leader, healer in those times had to be fire. She used hers. Lifting her sawed-off shotgun, she pointed it directly at the men challenging her leadership. Harriet said these words: "I understand, my people, the ferocity of your fears. But we have been slaves far too long. We have lost the taste for freedom. But here, under cover of this black night, I'm fixin' to make an executive decision. Those who choose to stay in this life of suffering may do so. Otherwise, whoever wants to have freedom sing in their bones and dreams tonight, follow me. Tonight, my people, we fixin' to be free."

In every group of human beings who care deeply to do this healing work, in the right way and spirit, there must be those, of any title, willing to walk the group through their long night of fear into the astounding daybreak of freedom. There is no other way than directly through our fear. We should do this now, good souls, before we further lose the taste of freedom.

MOVE OUT OF FEAR

Fear is a place we have made our unnatural house. It can never be our home. In order to move out of fear, we have to do many of the things we do when we move out of our residential home. We need to identify a new home. Let's call our new home *faith*. So we want to move out of fear into faith. We need to know faith's address, where to find it. Once we go there, we need to look around the neighborhood and the residence itself. To make sure it's really where we want to move. We take time to learn its quirks and subtleties.

Once we are decided, time to go back and start packing. It is vital that we are clear about what belongings are a part of our true self and the new life or work reality we desire. We don't want to move anything that isn't truly us into our new home. Any change brings grief, so we need to say goodbye to fear. Have a ceremony.

No use being grim about the whole thing. Have fun with it. Laugh and cry. Just make it clear to fear that you don't intend to move back in. It helps if your colleagues and formal leaders all decide to move out of fear together. That way you get to share the journey and encourage each other.

Some people will want to stay behind in the old neighborhood. Be careful that in visiting them, you don't end up living back in fear. The more time you spend in your new home, your true home, faith, not fear, the more at home you will feel. Start inviting people over. Your workplace is full of people who would Love to party at your new home, it's just that some of them have hardly ever ventured out of their house of fear. Entice them. Invite them over. Show them all the amenities faith has to offer. Show them the backyard and front yard, all the freedom. Show them the floor-to-ceiling windows, the stunning views, and the great plumbing and water pressure. Soon, you'll have others looking to make their own move. And when you feel a relapse coming on, use your mantra on yourself: *I choose to live in faith, not fear. I've got a brand new home.*

SCHOOL

What exactly are we preparing people for as they study to earn degrees for a career serving vulnerable human beings? Are we preparing them to process paperwork, fill out forms, and lead others through the same monotony? Are we shaping them to be agents for maintaining the social status quo so polluted with oppression and inequality? Or is our educational objective to nurture and foster professionals capable of genuinely supporting people in times of need? What do our professional degrees represent? Readiness to conform, burrow, and seek shelter? Availability to be used up and churned out by an uncaring system? It would be wonderful if our degrees reflected a qualification to be human in times of human crisis. Agents of actual social change, not only carrying skills but also eyesight, vision, a way of seeing the greatness in people and clear blue promissory skies in dire seasons of smoke and smog.

Curricula, syllabi, textbooks, lectures, homework... what is it all for? What are we creating here? We have agreed to something, or else we wouldn't continue with decade after decade of rolling out students into our professional fields. To what have we agreed? This is not an indictment of our educational programs, but a caring assertion that we need to take much better care of our educational programs. We can pay greater attention to the relationship between education and profession. The humane readiness of our workers and leaders is a function of their childhood and their education. These streams determine how they participate in their livelihood.

Is it true that we cannot better prepare students and professionals migrated from other careers? Of course we can improve. All human strivings can be improved. So, where is our will to evolve? Educational programs exist that invest in preparing students to understand the use of compassion and caring as tools. Programs that fortify students to prevent, manage, and heal from stress and trauma. But the stories of these kinds of programs seem suppressed. We don't hear about them often in the winds of professional conversation. Clearly, these programs can serve as examples of how we might evolve our idea and practice of education.

People shouldn't have to leave school to get schooled in the art and craft of the work. Yes, there are internships and such. But the core stream within educational programs is where the illumination and preparation needs to happen. It is there that we can begin planting seeds that help students become conscious of the role of self-care and mutual care. And of the ongoing responsibility to eradicate our social prejudices toward those we serve. After all, system leaders we have today were once schooled. For better and for worse, they are ambassadors of their schooling. If we desire continued evolution in our workforce and leadership, let's do some gardening. Let's do it in the place where the early seeds of ideas about people and relationship, work and service, get firmly planted.

TRAINING VERSUS GROWING

Most agencies have training departments or offices. These units facilitate the professional development aspect for staff. The word *training* implies bringing people into line, into conformity with standards. This is useful for ensuring technical skillsets. Our K-12 educational system is a training system. It creates graduates who have test-taking, paper-writing skills, and who have digested a culturally homogenous body of information about the world. After being shaped by this 13-year training process, we may or may not go on to further vocational, college, and/or graduate training. In these programs and environments, we are again conditioned to receive information, utilize memory, and take tests.

As a professor, I had to work hard to help my graduate students understand that a graduate seminar was different from typical undergraduate classes to which they were accustomed. A graduate seminar expects students to come prepared to teach and stretch each other, and not just sit half-asleep in their chairs waiting for the professor to transmit knowledge. But many graduate students these days assume that they should exist and behave in the same way as they did as undergraduates. I had to explain that graduate school was supposed to be a transitioning experience into professionalism, in which they learned how to actively learn, take initiative, and be a leader. Some of them were so conditioned to being passive, that they sat there paralyzed as I placed group power and process in their hands. Some of them expected to be literally read to like small children. They resented being expected to take initiative. They felt something was surely wrong, since they were not being spoon-fed knowledge. Sound familiar?

When we arrive into this work, most of us have been well-trained by our educational cultures. Maybe not in particular areas of knowledge, but certainly in the personality of passive learning. As we move through our professional career, we see a pattern: Many of us struggle with the real-life demands of serving human lives in need or crisis. We are contending with a nonlinear, unpredictable, chaotic, emotional, and ever-changing reality. This is true of the people we serve and of our workplace. Being strong at taking tests and engaging in passive learning doesn't necessarily help us in work that requires a high degree of initiative, self-belief, critical thinking, resourceful thinking, conflict resolution, problem solving, emotion management, social facilitation, linguistic flexibility, process fluidity, critical decision-making, teamwork, leadership, ingenuity, vision, and resilience. None of these qualities is a central part of any of our mainstream educational cultures or processes. The result? Fearful, insecure, disempowered, paralyzed workers and leaders.

Maybe, in addition to training departments, we could also use *growing departments*. The mission of growing departments would be to instill in professionals a spirit, attitude, and habit of personal and professional growth. *Psychological services,* and, *healing services* would be offered. These growing departments would not focus on information sharing, but on nurturing people's relationship with themselves in the context of their work and calling. This growing culture would create spaces, experiences, and connections that foster inspiration, aspiration, exploration, and a joy for personal transformation. Creative spirit and enterprise would be developed, along with literacy in caring, compassion, healing, and wellness. We would learn together how to discover our passions, purpose, and calling, and how to translate that into work performance that benefits our organization and service communities.

Our growing departments can be all about overcoming fear, flourishing within change, clarifying identity, learning empowerment language, taking initiative, having vision beyond current reality; and understanding the psychology of leadership, servitude, and professional kinship. Growing departments or offices... just an idea, a brainstormed name. What matters is that we begin to try new ways of developing our human resources. This work tests us to the core, and demands we reach our potential. We have so much growing to do.

GROUP HARMONY

Do we really understand what it means to work together? Our culture is so hyper-individualistic and competitive that it can be difficult for us to remove these strains from the spirit of collective work. If we talk about this challenge, honestly, then old spirit will have a way of leaving us, making room for the new. Hopefully we are experiencing a painfully necessitated paradigm shift from individualism to wholeness (whole family, whole community, whole workforce). Wholeness creates synthesis between its parts, a symbiotic musicality.

The collective energy of a group can be seen as a form of music. It is tonal, rhythmic, cadenced, and has lyrical meaning. We can feel it when we step into the work environment: the vibration of sharp, flat, sweet, and sour notes. Each group or agency is a symphony of relationships. To enhance this symphony, each musician needs to be in tune with her or his instrument and part in the music. The more consistent this attention, the stronger the musician, and the more fruitful the symphony. Every person in your organization is a tuning fork. If you touch them gently, they will hum with their intrinsic frequency. Find the ones tuned to health and harmony. Make sure they are being used as tuning forks to tune the collective instrument that is your agency. Otherwise, your system will produce a discordance, a bunch of sour notes that strike both the community and workforce painfully.

Sometimes, we try too hard to tune (grow) ourselves on our own. If we would only open ourselves to grow as a group, the collective wave can make our personal growth so much easier. We also get into trouble when we fall too far into solitary problem solving, something that stress pulls us toward. Sharing, brainstorming, and bouncing ideas back and forth all release pressure from individuals, transforming it into creative group energy. Teamwork and morale go hand in hand. As teamwork improves, morale improves. Our social nature works like this. As teamwork deteriorates, so does morale. So to improve morale, rather than judging, shaming, and isolating those with low morale, it is useful to focus together on strengthening bonds and work spirit.

At times we assume a person means us harm when in fact she or he simply lacks understanding, or maybe misunderstood us. Respectfully let them know how they impacted you. Ask them if perhaps there has been a misunderstanding. Easier said than done, yes? But also, easier done than not doing it at all and reaping the consequences of toxic relationship.

As a group, ask this question: *What is it we do that hurts us?* Your answers will be your roadmap for healing and growing. Also ask: *What is it we do that helps us?* Your answers will be your roadmap for sustaining wellness.

We supercharge social interactions by celebrating and encouraging each other. Whether or not you are a formal leader, start difficult conversations with staff or peers by highlighting their superpowers, the ways in which they bless the group and those they serve. Then move gently together into the territory of things that need to change. Difficult conversations can become a relatively comfortable habit for a group. This requires safe spaces and language, which can only be arrived at through practicing difficult conversations. In these spaces, our capacity to disagree, see things differently, and journey to the root of issues is a matter of safety, reassurance, and repetition. When colleagues seem to be struggling with attitude or morale, ask, "Please, share with me, why are you here in this work?" This question can help them reconnect to their purpose, to reunion with their lifelong mission and ministry. As they reunion, stress and despair fall away in a great shedding of false ideas.

Creating group harmony, especially within a change initiative, is more successful when certain ingredients are added:

Continuous Celebration. Consistency, consistency, consistency. People feel something is sincere when it is not a token gesture, but an ongoing quality of the relationship.

Timely Rewards. People need to receive meaningful, timely social reward for efforts and achievements. Immediate reward has a strong effect on the stimulus-response conditioning. Delayed reward can create a sense that your efforts are not valued.

Eager Promotion of the Work. Work efforts and outcomes need to be promoted passionately rather than with minimal sincerity and enthusiasm. This sends a message to the community and to the workforce.

Set Superordinate Goals. If units and teams set superordinate goals that each group cannot reach without the contributions of the other groups, this encourages collaboration and relationship across groups.

Maintain Equal Social Power. Individuals need to feel they hold social power equal to others in their group. Groups need to feel they hold social power equal to other groups. Genuine equal power creates ownership, creative prosperity, and harmony.

SUGGESTION BOXES

Sometimes people offer suggestions to each other, and then they put up their emotional fists and box. Do not confuse this with a *suggestion box*. Suggestion boxes can help generate feedback flow. But they must be used effectively. People need to be sincerely invited to contribute to them. And people need evidence that suggestions are being considered and used. A suggestion box can be literal, physical. Or it can be digital, or verbal during a group meeting or process. Be creative in the methods. Sometimes anonymity is helpful for suggestion boxes, sometimes not. Talk about it. Honor everyone's sensitivities by caring to talk about it. Thoughtfully explain decisions the group arrives at. Not explaining decisions can feel to people like their ideas and therefore they themselves were disregarded. So, explain, explain, explain. Good suggestion?

PUBLIC SHAME

Sometimes a colleague does something horrible with the public trust we have been given, or due to stress and unwellness is neglectful. Maybe a child or adult is harmed, or worse. The media tells the story in a way that makes it seem that the accused is representative of all of us who do the work. Being who we are, we feel deep, intense pain. Guilt, shame, and remorse flood through us. A sense of betrayal. We grieve for the harmed ones and the harm done, but don't know where or when or how to do it, so it pushes up out of us irregularly, doing more damage. We're supposed to keep on trudging through our work. But being at work, and thoughts of work, triggers us. Maybe we knew the accused, or know colleagues who were accused. Whatever outrage and pain the public feels, we feel it in a very different, eclipsing way. That person was ours. The harm came from us. Who are we now? What were we before? We question our identity. A crisis of confidence unfolds. And the pain... the undiluted pain continues.

What are we to do with these experiences, inside ourselves, with each other? As with all pain in all families, only one way out exists if we choose healing: We must spend time with what has happened. We cannot abandon ourselves or each other. This is a time for drawing closer, for pulling the blanket tighter. We have a story to nurture. Not a public relations story. The story of our truth. Who are we beyond the harm that has been done? How can we grow without destroying ourselves with guilt or anger? What is to be learned? How do we prevent these moments? How do we protect goodness, feeling that we failed to protect goodness? Goodness, we hurt. The story of our journey forward is vulnerable in this moment. We cannot forget so much that forgetting becomes denial. We cannot remember so much that remembrance becomes a consuming trauma. We have to spend time with this story of ours, which is a fire, a torch we carry. For the sake of the ones we serve, we need to tend this fire, preserve it. And for our sake. For our sake.

STRESS MANAGEMENT

Did you know that some turtles and tortoises are said to live over 150 years? My theory is that this is because these turtle people practice a secret form of Zen. Just a theory.

If you are a supervisor or a manager, in many ways what you are supervising and managing is stress. Your staff's and your own. It is an intangible element in your team climate that shows up in very tangible ways. Staff and leadership have a great need to work together in learning how to minimize this ever-present factor in the work.

Under stress, we regress to childhood habits. Do you want Dr. Banner or the Hulk? The rampaging child or the composed adult? If we want the adult doing the work, then we are better off investing in stress reduction and stress management. In wellness and healing. Or we can just ridicule these subjects as marginal to the work, and continue reaping the chaos and depression of intentional dysfunction. We are fooling ourselves if we believe that tribes become unwell accidentally. This is always the result of choices. What we choose to invest in, and what we choose to ignore.

Here are some *de-stressing* thoughts:

Identify the Source. It is best practice for staff to learn how to track the root of their stress. Causes are often multiple. Regular, brief, mindful time spent reflecting on these causes can create an ability to quickly identify them.

Identify the Expression. Helping staff to be conscious and aware of how they express their stress is a powerful life and work skill. Every person expresses stress differently. Freaking out is not so good. It is contagious. But so is remaining calm. A team in tune with each other's expressions can be more supportive.

Identify the Impact. It is very beneficial to staff to learn to be aware of how their stress expression affects those around them, impacts the work, and results in a self-damaging loop. Communication on this should be done in a caring manner.

Remove Stress Factors. Some stress factors are unavoidable within the work. Others can be removed. Have staff spend time thinking critically and creatively about even subtle changes they can make that will lessen the influx of stress.

Install Stress Busters. As a team, and personally, identify practices that break up stress. Think of stress as an invisible cloud that infiltrates a person, office, or building. Simple things like humor, deep breathing, brief meditation or reflection, storytelling, walking, music, and even a smile can all effectively dissipate clouds of stress. Stress clouds are always building. Stress busters blow those clouds away.

Role Model. Show your staff by your attitude, actions, and presentation how you are practicing stress management. Make it a supportive team commitment. Appoint calmness ambassadors.

Take Attendance. Together as a team, learn to take attendance on how stress is showing up in the work. No judging or criticism, just supportive testimony. Being honest about your stress and stressful situations is a primary tool. Verbalization releases stress, allows others to pitch in and help address your situation. "How are we doing?" This is a powerful question to ask regularly. It is a therapeutic, care-conveying question that tunes us in to our condition. Use this question informally and in meetings. It's like a yoga pose that creates awareness of our social body.

Celebrate Progress. Make sure to highlight calmness, peace, and positivity. Share the story of how you arrived at each of these. Teach other groups within your larger tribe what methods are working for you. Reward people for their progress. Ritualize your group's new stress flushing language, values, and behavior.

TIME FACTORS

Saying, "I don't have enough time for that," and not doing anything at all, is like saying, "I don't have enough money for the food I need," and then not eating at all. The *not enough time* declaration may reflect some measure of truth. It is also almost always a statement of attitude and perception. A chosen stance against trying something, or even opening to it.

One of the classic rationales that people use when they are resistant to change, or to a new idea, is to claim that they "don't have time for this." They will say things like, "Sounds good in theory, but we don't have time for this." The reality is that people will drown in their chaos, dysfunction, and trauma before ever grabbing hold of a change, even a small one that could keep them afloat, or better yet, get them on solid ground. Such is human nature.

Another reality is that there is no such thing as change without investing in time. Or, at least without investing in the time necessary to reflect on that change. And further, no tool or strategy exists that doesn't take time to implement on an organizational level. So the idea that a person or group doesn't "have time" to make change is the equivalent of saying, "We forever refuse to change, no matter how helpful it might be."

One of the things that people often fail to account for, in their devoted resistance to change, is the time that is lost by willfully holding onto ways and attitudes that aren't working. Here are just a few time-loss factors created by workplace, worker, and leader unwellness, and by the absence of mutual care:

Time lost to disempowered staff. Time lost to unaddressed stress, anxiety, fear, and trauma. Time lost attending to staff in crisis or conflict. Time lost to low morale (slow pace of work, negativity, errors, etc.). Time lost to staff exhaustion, burnout, and disillusionment. Time lost to poor task completion that needs to be revisited. Time lost to mediocre work ethic. Time lost to poorly served families. Time lost to miscommunication and misunderstanding. Time lost to insufficient teambuilding. Time lost to poor self-care and unwellness, and not just to sick days. Time lost to rushed and faulty case management, program planning, and mission strategizing.

Think about your own life and how much more efficient you are with time when you are well-rested, centered, present, in balance, clear-minded, focused, in a good mood, motivated, and purposeful. Whatever flow you just imagined is exactly why and how workplace wellness saves time and blesses the work. For example, time and celebration are both psychological phenomena: functions of perception, regardless of reality. This means that we can use them however we wish, as tools in our work. The more we celebrate, mentally, personally, or socially, the more time slows down. Refine this art and you are likely to find yourself right on time.

TIME *MANAGEMENT*

Time management is a popular topic and yet greatly misunderstood. Time is not to be managed. It is unmanageable. And certainly we do not manage time by working harder. Most people work too hard. They are literally killing themselves. What can be managed is the way we exist in our work. Our inner state, attitudes, expectations, and wellness habits influence the way we experience time. No one yet has succeeded in adding minutes to the clock by working harder, or being more stressed. But working peacefully and diminishing stress allows us to be more present, clear-minded, and skilled during the minutes available to us. Being in the moment mindfully, time slows, expands. Be in that same current anxiously, distractedly, and time contracts, flees swiftly.

One reason we struggle with time is because we relate to it rigidly while life itself is far from rigid. It is fluid, mercurial, spontaneous. But with time, we schedule things. We plan things. Humans can be very controlling and anxious when it comes to time. Possessive even. But when life happens, as it always does, it throws off our precious planning and we panic. If we learn a work culture that allows for spontaneity in changing course, we can take a great deal of pressure off ourselves.

An essential tension exists between time and job expectations. This can feel like a daily race. Some jobs feel this way more than others. But the anxieties of the race are there, lurking, for all of us. Examine how you experience time. Notice the thoughts that create anxiety. Work to cull those thoughts from your mental habit. Notice the thoughts that bring calm. Invite more of them to come. Share story regularly with each other and with leadership, about expectations and how they impact you. This is not a story of complaint but of construction. Build a way forward together that honors time and expectation both.

SOCIAL ISOLATION

Certain staff tend to feel socially isolated and devalued within agencies. For instance, IT staff. Administrative support staff. Facilities management staff. Their role and physical placement can be dehumanizing. Include them in social gatherings and celebrations that traditionally include only particular staff. It is easy to make people feel excluded. This affects their work and relationship with other staff. It is also easy to make people feel included. Just include them. In announcements, invitations, and events. They are an invaluable part of the team. Make them feel that way.

People who work in, let's say, Accounts Receivable, are exposed to an ongoing current of despairing, even angry calls. They may feel like they're hurting people, not helping them. This guilt and ambivalence is a form of trauma. Take care of this trauma by nurturing the wound. Encourage staff in these kinds of roles to share with each other as a peer group how they are impacted by their unique experiences. Have the larger agency acknowledge and express appreciation for this particularly difficult work they do. The idea is to not let them languish in a social vacuum, feeling as though no one understands or appreciates what they have to contend with. Wrap them in affirming story and attention, regularly, because their exposure is absolutely regular. Reassure them that they are helping people, and that they have an opportunity to affirm clients in compassionate tone and spirit, even as they perform their duty.

And if you are one of these isolated or highly exposed people, however you have been caring for yourself, care more deeply. After toxic phone calls, practice peaceful pauses, deep breathing, stretching, and unprovoked laughter. Dare to be seen acting crazy. Introduce yourself to people working outside your area. Share your stories humorously in writing, via newsletters and other forums. Advocate for your sanity. You may just rescue the sanity of a peer.

DISSOLVE SILOS

If you have ever driven through any agricultural region, you are likely to have passed through miles and miles of crops. *Cornfields...* This is the image that comes to me. And throughout that endless sea of harvest, you may have seen towering silver silos standing majestic amidst the growing bounty. Silos are for storing seed and grain. That seed and grain is not meant to stay in the silo forever. Any farmer knows this, and understands the intimate relationship between silos and crops.

In our work, too many agencies exist as a series of silos. All the seed and grain, the human ingenuity, talent, experience, and giftedness remain in the silos that are teams, units, branches, divisions, and departments. Extreme territoriality is at play. People—conditioned by unhealthy impulses of their work tribe— react to stress and trauma by becoming possessive, closed, and adversarial with other silos and their workers. We think and behave as though we are in a grand competition within the agency. We grow primitive, huddling behind our silo walls, thrusting arrows and spears of disregard and antipathy at the *dreaded others*. History has shown that we will fall into this *Us vs. Them* mentality in an instant. Give us something to distinguish ourselves from each other and the combat is on. In our work, the pressures and exposure of servitude combine with our human attraction for conflict and prejudice, and silos grow quickly.

We embrace these silos as though they are real. We aren't talking about different buildings or job duties here. We're talking about the social manufacturing of intense prejudice toward others simply because they work in a different group than we do. But there is a jeopardy to this silo effect: The human talent, tenor, and stories huddling together in each silo are seeds and grain. This seed and grain is meant to be shared with the rest of the tribe, the seed so that crops can grow, the grain so that souls can be fed. The purpose of silos on farms is to feed, not to starve. To create abundance and continuity. Without the dissemination of what is stored in the silos, there would be no crops, or anyone to eat them.

The higher purpose of silos in an agency or system is to feed the workforce, not to starve it. To create and share abundance of spirit, wisdom, insight, creativity, and continuity of culture and values. We humans are strange, and so we take bureaucratic designations, organizational structure, and we turn it into a battleground even though no one asked us to go to war. We are all one system serving the same children, adults, families, and communities, supposedly under the cultural banner of one mission. But we mutate job designations into fierce boundaries and deep prejudices, to the point that we won't even invite other groups to our office parties. What madness is this?

Our silo prejudices generate mythological tales about what other groups are doing, not doing, should be doing. We complain about what amenities they get and we don't get. We turn hearsay into hyperbole, as a nervous reaction to our stress and insecurity. We don't really know these other groups. How can we? We don't spend real time with them, and when we have an opportunity to create tribal time together, during which we can learn from and nourish each other, we reject the idea altogether, saying, "They don't belong with us. I don't see the reason for us to get together. It would just feel forced." But most new work relationships feel forced. They are the result of structure and mission, not the happenstance of running into each other at the grocery store.

If we give relationships a chance to happen, if we choose to dissolve psychological silos in our tribe, something organic occurs: *knowing each other*. And from this space of knowing, understanding sprouts. The seeds and grain of your silo get mixed with the seeds and grain of other silos, and before you know it, you have crops. A growing harvest. We dissolve silos by spending time together, and by challenging our prejudices and self-erected boundaries. Of course, we could just continue working on barren land, but no fruitful servitude exists in such a desolate vacuum.

To cross-fertilize your agency and dissolve silos, initiate a practice of staff and leadership making personal and group visits to other units, programs, divisions, and outside vendors and providers. This is a form of staff and leadership development that happens through positive social exposure.

Advocate for your various silos to socialize together more. Use the gatherings to learn from and feed each other. Share success stories and tales of what is working for your group, how you are resolving certain challenges, how you are managing certain people. For workers with low morale, confidence, or who seem to lack purpose, have them testify to these outside groups about what their group is doing or learning. When people are placed in a position to represent their group, it creates personal and group pride, ignites purpose. And when groups spend time together, natural mentoring is initiated across job boundaries. Our own group can grow stale if we never open the windows. Dissolving silos lets in fresh air.

Remember that childhood game, Red Rover, with two groups standing across from each other on the playground? *Red Rover, Red Rover, send so and so on over...* Someone needs not to wait to be sent, but to just take the initiative to go on over. After the first person takes the plunge, the dear and impressionable herd will follow.

BUILD RELATIONAL SPACES

Chronic stress can easily lead us into an attitude orientation in which we believe that most of our work experience is out of our control; that the stress and suffering and chaos are simply a fact of the work. This false narrative is a powerful factor in the progression of the trauma and dysfunction that damage our capacity to operate at an optimal level. A potent dynamic exists as a tonic for this defeatist attitude: *relationships*. Relationships are one of our most empowering commodities. Our capacity to foster them exists within us, independent of our work conditions.

A relationship requires no fiscal funding, no permission from external authority, no policy directive or strategic initiative, and in many ways is not dependent upon the availability of time. This is because the essence of relationship lies in the mind, heart, and spirit; those perceptual spaces that are ours alone. Relational spaces do not only exist between people. Music is a relational space. The question is, do you practice fortifying that space? Art, good books, dancing, singing, crying, laughing, bonsai, meditation, smiling, hiking, and traveling: all are relational spaces. Healthy relational spaces open us. To ourselves. So that both the beauty and pain inside can flow out. And so that what is externally nutritional can flow in.

Just as relationships hold so much promise as a nurturing, healing, resolving, enlightening, and comforting resource, they also require a home. A space in which the relationship can grow and thrive. This is what is meant by the term *Relational Space*. We are reassured knowing that someone cares about us, thinks about us, and wishes us well. A relational space can be in full effect even when we are not physically interacting with that person. It is a sense of knowing. A harboring of shared experience, memory, values, stories, hopes, and intentions. Human beings are intensely social animals. Relational spaces are our territory. But they must be maintained. The most dysfunctional workplaces are drought stricken. Relational fluidity has dried up. Workers and their vital caring spirit have shriveled.

We must continuously build relational spaces, because life and stress are always eroding these spaces. Such spaces feel safe to those inside them, and foster trust, openness, communication, and the intimacy required for tribal wellness.

The vast majority of helping professionals succumb not to the realities of their work, but to the contraction and constriction of their own hearts under duress. Relational spaces are dilation valves. They keep us open. Breathing. Flowing. In nature, rivers deliver rich sediment that feed estuaries and oceans. Relational spaces deliver to us the fertility of being cared for. Of being recognized, acknowledged, heard, validated, celebrated, and honored. To minimize all of this as triviality is a culturally blind attitude at the root of our system and societal disintegration. We are falling apart.

Not because of human suffering. That has always been with us. We fall apart because of the erosion of our relational spaces and our failure to give ourselves to them. These are matters of physics, chemistry, biology, and physiology, just as much as they are matters of psychology and emotionality. We are designed and wired to be open and to flow, to pour out and to be poured into.

THE LANGUAGE OF *WE*

The language of *We* is a very powerful language. When it becomes your tribal language, it helps people evolve their identity from individualistic to collective. This in turn, fosters a change in the culture from territorial, competitive, and combative, to communal and reciprocal. Too much language of *I* creates intensely self-serving culture. Trust and safety evaporate. So start a campaign. Practice using *We* in regular operational communications, staff meetings, newsletters, and event promotions. Use *We* in your team's rituals and traditions. Speak *We* when you are expressing a personal need or concern. See what effect it has over time.

How does this benefit me? This is a question we are always asking ourselves on a primal, survival level. If we redefine the *Me* to include *We*, we awaken the communal spirit that drives all healthy tribes. The language of *We* conditions people from identities of the small self to the large self. We literally redefine the boundary of who makes up *Us*, and *I*, extending the perimeter wider and wider. This matters because we are strongly motivated by self-interest. Redefine the self and you empower *We-interest*. Children use *I* because they are scared and insecure in this overwhelming world. We are no longer children. *We* comes from a place of maturity and security, and creates an aura of safety benefitting everyone.

BUILD A TRIBE
(The next evolution beyond teambuilding)

The term *team* can imply competition and boundaries. A tribe exists for relationships and communal purpose. We build tribes not through titles and territories, but through intimacy and reciprocity.

Strong, vital, resilient tribes possess certain qualities. Building such a tribe is not as much about the personalities involved, as it is a commitment to creating safety, harmony, and role fit. Tribe building in times of turnover and change can be difficult. Then again, when is it not a season of turnover and change? Change itself is an opportunity to strengthen your tribe. Focus on what is actually being lost, what is being perceived as lost, and what is being gained. Honor and share grief, sorrow, and fears of the unknown. Grow closer, not more distant. Wrap the blanket tighter. Reappraise roles and opportunities. A new season is upon you. Nurture each other into it. Here are some ingredients:

Safety. A primary need for human beings is to feel safe. Our time in the womb is often our template for ultimate safety. Anything less can create anxiety, and in some, a tendency to panic. Panic is not so good. It causes us to close and hide, rather than open and shine our light. Safety factors are unique for each person. This calls for caring, nonjudgmental conversation and exploration of these factors, so that we can work toward collective safety. Safety isn't the absolute impossibility of harm, but the likelihood and expectation of consideration, sensitivity, protection, and support.

Safety isn't a standard. It is a phenomenon each person does or does not experience. To increase the likelihood that each person experiences safety, safety needs to be a priority in your group's ongoing story. Manifesting safety is a creative act dependent upon the gathering of stories, and caring enough to make changes. Small changes increase safety. Like opening up communication and conversation. Inviting each person to contribute to the safety story and initiative. Sharing lessons without judgment leads to safety. As does treating people in the same way that makes *you* feel safe when you are treated that way. See? More mutuality. Yes, safety emerges from cultures of mutuality. Quite naturally.

Harmony. To counteract cultural pressures toward competition, individualism, and conflict, harmony needs to actually be practiced, until it becomes cultural. Harmony is not perfect peace. It is a devoted attitude of mutual support, care, relationship investment, and movement in the same direction toward overarching goals.

Superpowers. We each have natural superpowers that likely haven't been tapped, nurtured, or celebrated throughout life. No one wrote a comic book or graphic novel about our superpowers. Our work together, and the stories told, must be that graphic novel. It is critical to identify each person's superpowers so that staff can be placed into roles that fit, independent of their formal job titles. Role fit is a key aspect of a strong tribe.

Relationship Priority. A healthy, vibrant, fruitful tribe values relationship over task. *People before process* is a magical mantra. It makes wellness suddenly appear. People and relationships are not commodities. They are foundations that allow work resources and commodities to be maximized.

Testimony and Bearing Witness. In order to feel safe, people need to feel that when they express or testify to their experience, no matter how small or insignificant, they can trust that their tribe will somehow bear witness: Listen, empathize, relate, support.

Taming Fear. This is an important aspect of creating a sense of safety. Fear must be freely acknowledged, talked about, and addressed so that people learn they have power over their fear. Practice doesn't make fearless. It makes fearsome.

Representing. Place staff in opportunities to represent the tribe, within the agency and within the community, and watch pride, morale, and appreciation for the work blossom. Representing, in presentations, written communications, and creative projects, causes a person to have to learn more about their tribe, taps appreciation for the tribe, and exposes the person to the insights and perspectives of other tribes.

ABORIGINAL ROLE WISDOM

Aboriginal people of Australia have learned over many centuries the importance of roles in maintaining the integrity and fabric of a group. Their indigenous wisdom allows them to create and preserve tight social bonds even in this modern age of individualism and encroaching materialism. Here, community members pay intimate attention to one another in order to discern gifts and interests, and how these traits might be useful in certain group roles. If this practice seems familiar, it is because it is a tradition practiced also by the Diné people and other Indigenous cultures. Aboriginal culture understands that without each person manifesting her or his full potential and calling, the people will ultimately perish. This makes role-taking essential.

Through attentive relationship, people are guided by their elders into recognizing the roles that are meant for them. Their role is not determined by academic major or degree, but by personal nature and giftedness. When someone in a particular role passes away or is otherwise lost to the community, that role is filled not just to fill the space. The role is filled only when a person with the right nature and giftedness is identified. Role assignment is not a bureaucratic procedural. It is a spiritual and social practice of preservation. People don't feel devalued in their work because the ongoing cultural conversation is endlessly affirmative: *We need you to be you in order for us to be us.*

Role assignment in our organizations can be facilitated in a similar fashion. Create graphic representations of the web of relationships and roles that make up your team, unit, or tribe. Have conversation, regularly, about each person's nature. This is honoring, affirming conversation, even if the subject is traits that might not be socially desirable in the broader world. Take the conversation along its course until each person is able to get her or his story out into the atmosphere.

Some people are good at forming relationships. Have them form a relationship team. For you, actively find roles that suit your personality. Have others do the same. So-called overachievers and underachievers have a purposeful place in your group. What do you do with them? How do you use them? The answers come from asking them how they would like to be used. And from exploring possibilities together as a group.

As people grow familiar with each other's personal nature and passions, continue graphically refining the portrait of your group's formal and informal task roles. Define these roles not in bureaucratic language, but in a language of traits and personas. As with an art project, keep messing with the paints and colors. Keep matching, shifting, and placing.

Make sure that role functions are clear to all, and that each role assignment creates a harmony between who the person is and what the role function is. Your clowns have a precious role in the group, to keep people laughing, a great medicine and tension-flushing instrument. You have so-called introverts and extroverts, intellects and artists, tech-savvy and numbers people, visionaries and detailers, multitaskers and highly focused souls. Some Love to socialize, others to rationalize (your Spock people). Some have a passion for learning, others are bookworms, and then there are those who provide a good shoulder to lean on. Everyone has a personal nature, and every personal nature has something to offer within the right role.

In human groups, there will forever be people who do more than their share of the work, and those who spend great energy finding ways to *pass the buck*. Allow each person to select distinct tasks to fulfill. Celebrate their task-role at this point of selection. This isn't premature celebration. It is initiative celebration, which increases people's sense of duty and public commitment to the task.

Allow people to grow into their ongoing group roles. Let staff identify a competency from a list of team duties, and then practice it. And instead of continuing to use the same old formal roles (sometimes out of nothing more than habit), let us invite informal, *soul roles* that inspire people in their work, affirming their worth and celebrating their story. Indigenous cultures have something to teach us about what it means to work together, and in working together, nurturing healing and wellness in each of us.

In the tradition of many African cultures, it is recognized that each of us is born with a song, and that it is the role of the family and community to recognize, practice, and celebrate this song. The song is a literal and symbolic representation of each person's purpose in the world, in their work. We need not decide for a worker what his or her song is. The song is theirs to determine. Some have arrived all the way into adulthood and far into their career without discovering their song. Their team or unit has an opportunity to inspire and bring out into the work this person's song. Instead of suppressing people's nature, shaping them into a conforming, indistinct group of workers, we can encourage their unique nature out into the open, where we can learn from it, diversify our team, and strengthen our mission. We'll be singing as we go.

SUPERPOWERS

I was comic book crazy as a child. I stayed up late at night with a flashlight under the covers reading story after story. Looking back, I realize that part of what I was attracted to was the relationship the characters had with their own unique personal traits. Almost all of the superheroes had something about them that they initially thought of as a bad thing. Society told them that their uniqueness made them freaks of nature. Mutants. Outcasts and monsters. Unsafe and undesirable for society. This caused the characters to internalize their sense of not belonging. Many of them grew self-destructive. Then came their saving grace. One way or another, usually through the mentoring of another outcast, they came to realize that what made them different was not only not a bad thing, but it was their *superpower*. Their distinctive traits were actually a giftedness for their true calling and purpose in life. As soon as they realized this, their relationship with themselves changed. They stood taller, didn't allow others to abuse them. They were more Loving, inwardly and outwardly. They had found their place and sense of belonging. These characters had gone from being outcasts to being superheroes.

It works like this in real life, too. Until you and I do the deep inner work of realizing the purpose of what makes us unique, we are likely to continue manifesting negative self-ideas planted in us during childhood. This greatly affects our work. We have a very important question to ask ourselves: *What is my superpower?* Make this a staff exercise. Even though it may lighten the mood, and receive ridicule and laughter, take the exercise earnestly. People come into this work and hit the ground running. Being tasked with difficult caseloads and crises, we barely stop to ponder what it is that we have to offer to the team, and those we serve.

Maybe you grew up with no one in your life recognizing or celebrating your superpowers. You would be far from alone. Think of traits that may be devalued by society. Can those same traits somehow be of benefit in your particular work duty? Don't run away from the parts of you with which you are uncomfortable. Focus on those in particular. How can you use your born nature or acquired persona to be of help here in your vocation? As a team, take your superpowers seriously. Don't start leaping around the office in capes and leotards. Or, do. It might be helpful. But make superpower stuff a part of your regular teamwork. Talk and laugh about what you each uniquely bring to the mission. Celebrate it. When new team members arrive, invite them to explore their superpowers. Introduce them to each team member's special power. This breaks the ice and strengthens bonds. And when team members leave, recognize together the superpowers that have been lost. This awareness helps your group replenish and evolve itself, staying strong.

ROLE FIT

How does who you are fit into your assigned role? Each of us needs to ask this question. If we don't, we are contributing to role misfit within our group or tribe. Role misfit can be more destructive to a group than not having roles filled at all. People are too often promoted into leadership positions because of a need to fill a space, or because of how they performed in another role, without role-makers ever considering how those people might fit as leaders. We tend to assume promotion is a good thing. But if people are not by nature a good fit for, or ready for their new role, then promotion is counterproductive for the person, the group, the system, and the community. Promotional criteria matter, as does adhering to those criteria. Work with people to make sure they are accepting a promotion for the right reasons. Recognize promotion as a season of change, loss, and gain, a point of personal and group vulnerability that we can pay attention to and support. Promotion creates significant social and operational ripples through the tribe. Let's pay attention to those waves as well.

Workers avoid promotion fearing the unknown, fearing added responsibility. Yet, they may be better suited for a leadership position than they are for their current position. And what of traits? *Extroverts, introverts, high energy, focused, scattered, creative, analytic, linguistic...* We misuse and underuse these identifiers in our work. Assumptions are made about what each type means in various roles. Without deeper examination, personally and collectively, we may be missing the opportunity for someone to find a niche that sets them on fire with passion and giftedness, and blesses the tribe.

MENTORING

Our idea of mentoring is tired and worn out. It needs respite care. First of all, we can be much more creative about how we pair up people in mentoring relationships. Organic beginnings are great, we can encourage people to pair up informally, spontaneously, creatively. I am not advocating some kind of dating game within the agency or program, but we could treat mentoring with much more joy and fun. And we can tell the story of our group's mentoring relationships creatively. This is a role modeling opportunity.

We can also allow ourselves to connect beyond structural job boundaries. Someone who cleans the floors and windows surely has some great perspective and wisdom to offer an agency director. So, less ego, more humility and grace. Our mentoring culture needs to be less serious and linear. Task-oriented mentoring is great, but life is not linear, it is chaos. We don't need to treat mentoring like a dreary case of classroom teaching. Transferring information from one person to another is helpful, but two people sharing and supporting each other in a spirit of creativity and fun, this is fruitful. Less of the rigid teacher-student arrangements, and more of the intuitive "These two crazy people might actually be good for each other" approach.

We need mentoring for our mentoring. Instead of shoving people into each other and saying, *Go mentor,* how about we talk about mentoring as part of our staff meetings and development? The word means different things to each person. Be honest about your mentoring needs. Don't wait for someone to suddenly offer you mentoring. During tribal gatherings, formal meetings, or in passing in the hallway, ask for help or guidance. We encourage our children to ask questions in class and approach their teachers for help, and in college to advocate for what they need, but we are so often passive about our same needs. Maybe we are afraid. We're supposed to be professionals, right? We don't want to acknowledge our need for help or guidance, because we're afraid we'll be seen as incapable, unqualified. So, then, fear needs to be a part of what we talk about in our mentoring culture and process. Fears of those who need mentoring, fears of those who should be mentoring.

Relationships, when healthy, are mutual creatures. We have treated mentoring as a one-way street. This creates condescension, discomfort, and obstructed flow. Let's open up the channels, and invite ourselves to feed each other reciprocally. Everyone has something for someone. Symbiosis is a good word.

KINSHIP GROUPS

If you plant kinship groups in the soil around your agency, they will bear many fruits. We use the term *kinship* here to distinguish it from the idea of peer group, support group, or affinity group. Kinship is a warm relationship that includes formal peer aspects, as well as support and affinity. Kinship is a binding of roots, an active interweaving of causes and intimacies. Grant your kinship groups the freedom to gather formally and informally. Face-to-face and otherwise. Allow them to develop organically. Encourage and celebrate their emergence. They will evolve their own traditions for being together. Ensure these stories are told throughout the agency or larger group. Mix levels of authority together in some kinship groups. A secretary can be a great mentor for a director. A caseworker can bless a manager. Create peer-level groups as well.

Treat these kinship groups as learning circles. Whether for so-called front-end or back-end services, it is the learning aspect that cements group bonding and personal and professional growth. We share together because it feels good. And also because we become something new.

The focus of your kinship groups is not work-tasking, per say. It is simply relationship richness, knowing that work tasking naturally arises from this kinship ground. People need intimacy. Whether as teenagers on a college campus, or at work, the more disconnected and isolated we feel, the more overwhelmed we become. The larger or more frantic the organization or system, the more value kinship groups hold. They are where we grow centered, secure, and fed, so that we can better tackle the broader wilderness of what we do.

Fruitful service organizations hold ongoing space and process for testimony and bearing witness. People feel safe sharing socially about the challenges and blessings of their work reality. They know their testimony will be honored. That something will be done with it to make the group stronger and the work more effective. They trust that their peers, including leadership, will bear witness, meaning that they will be listened to constructively (in order to construct) and without judgment. Testimony and bearing witness, also referred to as *Truth and Reconciliation*, is a greatly validated method for healing wounds within and between groups, and for facilitating group cohesion (teambuilding).

This reciprocal act is all about the medicinal power of acknowledgement, one of the roots of healing. Acknowledgement to the self and by others is an act of being seen. Being seen is a primal human need. *Seen*, as in recognized, valued, and embraced. In your service work, testimony and witness helps to set group roles and cultures. It is a ritualized way of saying, "This is our history, our journey, our pain and passion, our purpose, and our path forward." Without a sincere priority on and space for testimony and witness, formally and spontaneously, conflicts between people and groups fester and become more dominant than the work itself. Once people are finally allowed to express themselves, the pain and hurt comes spewing out in destructive geysers, rather than in honoring tones and language. Few are able to listen and openly receive what feels like an assault, and so the very people who need to bear witness close up, protectively.

Paired together, testimony and witness is a release valve for any pressure resulting from the work and from social disharmony. It is not a process marginal to the work. It allows the flourishing of servitude. You can think creatively with each other about how to build a strong tradition of testimony and witness. As with all things, we need practice to learn how to communicate with each other in nurturing ways, so that all of us, regardless of position, can feel, *I am seen, here. I am seen. I am known.*

Formal leaders play a critical role in facilitating clear language and idea clarity within a group. Leaders need to be tuned into their own language, ensuring that what they think their language means is the same meaning that staff will interpret from their language. Often, not enough care is taken in this measure. Confusion and misunderstanding ensue, resulting in rebellions against change initiatives that were never given a fair opportunity to be understood.

If we define leadership as a phenomenon (rather than a person) inspiring both work and culture, relationship becomes paramount. A phenomenon is a happening. A dynamic. This kind of leadership is not a person, title, or position. It is an energy and spirit that prevails, affecting work and climate. Thus, the relationship between the social health of a workforce and its service to a community is a function of what kind of leadership phenomenon is happening.

Are we concerned with transformative service delivery that inspires new ways of existing in children, adults, and families? Or are we satisfied with basic service delivery? If we care for life to improve for all, our leadership phenomenon (or rather, our constellation of leadership phenomena) needs to have a certain persona to it. Inspired leadership cares about particular things in its staff and workplace. *It cares about creating a spirit of accountability, an attitude of ownership, an "altitude" of compassion, and an aura of relationship.* These are its operational priorities, recognizing that fiscal health and quantitative outcome validation arise from a climate in which people care deeply enough. About themselves, each other, their leadership, and those they serve. And that people are equipped with the attitudes and skills to nurture these relationships.

As we continue to define leadership, we ask: *Who is leading?* The true answer: *All of us.* Leadership is a collective spirit residing in relationships, not individuals, and actualized through story. We are a constellation of phenomena, each with our own giftedness and expression, bound and kindred by a priority of common caring that we be well, that our service be nurturing and honoring, and that communities heal and are empowered.

What are we leading? Not people, but ideas, spirit, and vision. We are gardening a way of seeing and being, into which people are placed and come to thrive.

What is the outcome of all of this? Transformative service delivery that creates the following: healthier servant leaders and practitioners. Greater continuity of employment and system culture. Increased fiscal efficiency. The breaking of generational cycles of family and community dysfunction and disempowerment. Less human resource pressure on systems to meet community needs. Integration of systems into the community as a concentrated resource, rather than being a condescending and disconnected castle imposing itself on the community. Natural infusion of cultural relationship from the community into the system, and vice versa. Wholeness is our harvest.

TRANSPARENCY

Here is yet another fashionable concept these days. *Transparency.* People commonly seem to take this term to have to do with agency leadership telling staff everything about everything. Looking closer, we can see that people's call for transparency reflects a sense of disempowerment, devaluation, and lack of control over their reality. All three of these aspects can be addressed without necessarily communicating every aspect of administration. Empowerment, valuation, and a sense of control can be infused into staff in a multitude of ways, many of which we have already covered.

Transparency is also not exclusively about openness and sharing. More precisely, *it is a function of how and when sharing happens, and its spirit or intent.* Sharing, revealing, and explaining can land in a way that feels controlling, manipulative, and condescending. Similar to the way we all felt at times as children when our parents or other adults communicated with us. True transparency is about sharing, revealing, and explaining in a way that feels like authentic partnership. It should feel as though we are being shared with because the sharer wants and needs us to know, as a part of our role in the tribe.

Transparency is also not an exclusive responsibility of formal leadership. Staff have just as much duty to ensure that the way in which they share, reveal, and communicate with leadership feels honoring, and in a spirit of partnership and building together. This is a hallmark of mutual care: a group commitment to caring about the sharing aspect of relationship. A culture of practicing timely, intentional, thoughtful communication.

THE *WHY* OF TRANSPARENCY

The "Because I said so..." and "My way or the highway..." approach to leadership and making requests doesn't work so well. It may feel good to the ego, but what do you do when half of your workforce chooses the highway? Or when staff don't stay long enough to even get through the orientation process? "Because I said so" often doesn't work so well even parent-to-child. Certainly not between adults. This attitude, whether verbalized or not, conveys control, dominance, and condescension. It likely breeds fear and/or resentment. Whatever we fear, we come to resent.

You know those children who are always asking their parents, "Why?" Maybe you were one of them. Even for adults, knowing the *Why* to a request or change, is a way to manage anxiety about the unknown. Providing the *Why* can be much easier, quicker, and relationship-building than having to contend with the consequences of not providing the *Why.* Informed choice empowers people. Makes them feel respected and trusted. Notice the *choice* part of the phrase. Choice is how adults are made to feel that they have ownership of their work life. Deep down, no one wants to be owned. We want own to own our life and work.

FRUITFULNESS AND PRODUCTIVITY

Imagine a thriving orchard that bears sweet, succulent fruit season after season, year after year, no matter the conditions. An orchard so healthy, with all of its elements in harmony... that it virtually sings with vitality. Now imagine an orchard that produces fruit, but only because its workers labor so hard to get anything out of the poor soil, polluted water, decayed roots, and damaged trees that they themselves grow unwell, burnout, and leave. As soon as the workers are gone—workers who had to apply every ounce of their effort, skill, and giftedness just to harvest a few stunted fruits—the orchard immediately becomes barren. It produces no fruit. The first orchard described here is a fruitful orchard. The second orchard is temporarily productive, but not fruitful. For work tribes that serve human lives, productivity is not a high enough standard. *Fruitfulness* is what we are after. Here are some key differences between a productive agency and a fruitful one:

Productive organizations often depend heavily upon current conditions, workers, and leaders in order to achieve positive outcomes. *Fruitful* organizations can withstand changes in conditions, workforce, and leadership and still achieve positive outcomes.

Productive organizations may have low morale, negative conditions, imbalanced people, and unhealthy habits; but are able to overcome this to a degree and for a period by leadership based on fear, intimidation, punishment, and social sanctioning. Burnout eventually occurs on all levels. *Fruitful* organizations thrive through high morale, positive conditions, people in balance, and healthy habits; and enjoy leadership based on relationship building, positivity, staff empowerment, and staff ownership of the organizational culture.

Productive organizations often work within crisis but do not attend to crisis. *Fruitful* organizations exist in such a way as to prevent, heal, and learn from crisis.

Productive organizations may have climates in which staff identify rigidly with their title. *Fruitful* organizations have climates in which staff identify passionately with their gifts.

Productive organizations may be uninspired, uncreative, and consumed with existing processes and habits. *Fruitful* organizations are constantly creating, envisioning, imagining, daring, and striving. They have a passion for learning, growing, and transforming. These tribes are inspired by, not threatened by, community cultures, conditions, and changes.

Productive organizations may serve the community but rarely transform the community. *Fruitful* organizations create social fertility and inspire transformation in their community.

RETENTION AND FRUITFULNESS

Retention is a self-defeating standard that too many agencies set as their target. Retention is a low standard to keep, and rarely results in workers reaching their greatest potential. The psychology of retention results in systems doing just enough to keep people, but not nearly enough to nurture, grow, and inspire people. As a leader or staff, spend time working with your people on what makes them want to stay, instead of reacting to what makes people want to leave. Spend time together in the *garden of staying*. More people will want to stay.

Fruitfulness is a more useful standard than retention. Fruitfulness sees people at their best, doing their best work, not wanting to leave, and feeling fulfilled and affirmed. When we don't invest in fruitfulness as an umbrella that includes retention, we lose not only people, but also their entire life wisdom and story, their richness of soul and perspective. We lose their language, heritage, and instinct. We lose the rhythm and momentum of the relationships they had with workers and leaders left behind. All of this translates into fiscal loss, and operational jeopardy. We cannot afford to have people who were born to serve flood out the doors of this work for no other reason than that they themselves were not caringly served and nurtured. These people are our precious fruits. As their fulfillment multiplies, we are all left more fruitful.

START A MICRO REVOLUTION

People in systems, regardless of title, often become overwhelmed and intimidated by the idea of transforming the culture and climate. When this happens, it can be helpful to reduce the circle. Instead of considering the larger ecosystem, start with a comfortable, more intimate circle or parameter. First, of course, start with yourself. The next larger concentric circle may be your team or unit. A great way to stage a peaceful, lasting revolution of your system is by starting a micro revolution in your team. The relationships are already in place to a degree, and you have a somewhat captive audience. Advocate for your team to commit itself to a renovation project. A beautification project. What are the small, granular practice habits that each of you can pledge to role model? What are the collective practice habits that your team can commit to?

Involve each team member equally in terms of input and consideration. But start. Not starting is the most common failure characteristic of change. Each person, start. Take a stand and say, "This is what I am going to begin practicing. In my personal life. In my job role. In my work relationships." Encourage each other to keep adding ideas to the creative pot. Our creative muscle is critically atrophied when it comes to our system life. Too often we adapt a passive, enslaved, zombie persona, a disembodied way of showing up to work, daily repeating the mantra, *I have no power. There is nothing I can do to change my reality or the reality of this place. It is too big. I am too small. The situation is hopeless.* This kind of narrative is wonderful for dramatic effect. Not so effective for making things better.

So, start. Each of you. All of you together. Once you have started, make sure you are each recording and preserving the story in some way. You are going to need access to the story in order to extend your micro revolution beyond the team, out into the wild territory of the larger agency. Micro revolutions depend greatly on the broadcasting of story. Your team can be an exemplar, a role model for modest and courageous ideas and practices you are trying. At least your team is now trying. This striving itself is a story that other teams in your system need to hear and be pollinated with. Keep on assessing not only your project, but also your telling of it, which can always be made more effective. How is our language? Does it mean to others what it means to us? What does it mean to us? What are some new creative ways we can transmit our story?

Micro revolutions are a helpful way to start because they occur within smaller, more intimate spaces where story can more easily be shared. Think of how you start a fire in the wilderness. First, you gather your kindling. Once the kindling is ignited by a spark, you blow on the first flames. This breath is your storytelling as a team. When the flames are strong enough, you introduce larger twigs and branches to the fire. When the fire is ready, you add the big leaguers: the heavy logs that will sustain and hold the fire long-term. This is how you bring revolution from the kindling of self, to the next largest branch that is your team; and as you strengthen your project and its story, you bring your heat to the agency.

Along the way, you get better at blowing on the healing fires (and dousing the illness fires). Once the agency is on fire, now you can bring the revolution to the community in a way that feels honest and authentic to the community. This is imperative, for the community always holds the largest, most lasting fire. The people need to feel that your agency fire is worthy of joining with the community fire. Once these two fires join, you have the conditions for actually reversing the generational dysfunction and statistics that so frequently evade our best efforts.

So, start a revolution today. Someone needs to start the fire. Begin with the area over which you have the most control: yourself. Tell that story to your team, and together blow on the kindling of personal transformation and practice habits. Together, choose to be a micro revolution. One day, your team may become a legend in your system about how wellness and honoring servitude first became a fire.

SUSTAIN CHANGE

It is always a challenge to sustain and perpetuate any change once the initial process or initiative has been completed. Sustainability comes from shared accountability. The more mutuality there is in your culture of care, the more sustainable the culture. We look too often for technical strategies to create sustainability. But this peculiar creature lives inside of relationships. It goes where they go. To develop roots for lasting personal, group, and system cultural change, here are some strategies you can complement with your own:

Build the identified change principles into your personal and group traditions, habits, rituals, and processes. Create new traditions, habits, rituals, and processes that will internalize the changes and help the changes withstand personnel and leadership turnover and other unpredictable variables. Continuously promote and celebrate the values relevant to your change initiative. Create sustaining processes to ensure the incorporation, integration, and perpetuation of your change principles. This involves processes such as recruitment, hiring, orientation, ongoing development, and cultural maintenance. Identify torch-bearers (role models or exemplars) for the change principles. Have these torch-bearers regularly mentor promising new torch-bearers. Create and preserve storytelling modes and traditions that will promote, celebrate, and generationally extend change-related practices, values, and visions.

How often do we review our mission statements to see whether they are in harmony with our reality? This is a useful practice. Drift from ideals is natural, especially within high stress atmospheres. The only cure for drift is to first be aware of the drifting. Then it is a matter of getting back on course. For that, we need a vision, a strategy, ownership from all parties, and a commitment to practice.

Leaders come and go. It is a good idea to have a plan of succession. Some of the most useful succession plans aren't about identifying future leaders. The focus instead is on the transmission of leadership spirit and skills to the entire group. We never know the future of a group. If we invest in identifying future leaders, those people may or may not be around when the time comes for them to lead. Or maybe our assessment of them was not the most accurate. We miss seeing some of the most natural leaders. Inclusive leadership transmission can be a better bet than exclusive plans. Mutual care fertilizes an agency with formal leadership seeds in every worker. These seeds know when to sprout: when they are called upon.

Change is not sustained magically. It survives and thrives where language, process, structure, story, and celebration are in place to carry it forward until it is considered normal. Strong cultures endure brief and long absences from formal leaders, and changes in leadership. This is because values have become habits. Staff are activated leaders, taking over intuitively. When your tribe learns how to keep itself in harmony with its culture, now you know you are getting somewhere.

MUTUAL CARE AGREEMENT

All organizations make agreements. The majority of these are silent, unspoken, unwritten, and arrived at through fear and anxiety. Fruitful, thriving, safe organizations commit to making healthy agreements out loud. They paint their spaces with these agreements in multiple ways: in writing, graphically, creatively, procedurally, and ritually.

Advocate that your staff and management work in collaboration to develop a Mutual Care Agreement (MCA). An MCA is intended to articulate a code and culture for relationships between all employees, regardless of position. The MCA essentially asserts that: *Each employee is devotedly responsible for relating to his or her coworkers in a manner that is mutually nurturing, honoring, and supportive, regardless of level of authority.*

An MCA is a practice tool for creating and maintaining a culture of mutual care. Because its principles are rooted in mutuality, it is useful as both a short-term and long-term teambuilding instrument, and a powerful primer for a tradition of self-and-group care and wellness. The MCA should act as a communal challenge, a reminder, a checkpoint, a measuring stick, and a source of insight and inspiration. By continually reaffirming your agreements, your organization has a much better chance of carrying forward this renewal work. Use the MCA for lasting change, and to grow deep cultural roots.

A thoughtful MCA can empower staff and leadership in their respective roles, improve the partnership between staff and leadership, and create a healthier work environment. It can help increase sensitivity to people served, and to each other. Such a blueprint serves to minimize the effects of stress and trauma, and maximize tribal strengths, bonds, and wellness. Ultimately, the cultural practice of an MCA can result in a collective sense of trust and safety that does not disappear as leadership and staff come and go. It becomes the roots and soil of a healthy work ecology.

An MCA is meant to be amended freely and indefinitely over time as necessary. It is to be a living document. Perhaps start by having each unit develop its own MCA that they then share with the larger department or agency. In the agreement, highlight: (1) what the MCA is to be used for within the organization; (2) what organizational values will be committed to and practiced; (3) what the MCA objectives are in terms of organizational growth and improvement; and (4) the specific daily practice skills to be affirmed by the evolving agreement.

Each person should feel her or his input and imprint in the evolving agreement. And both the document and the process can be used during recruitment, hiring, orientation, ongoing staff and leadership development, and for inspiring change within larger related systems. The MCA becomes your story of how your agency continues to become a more compassionate, nurturing, fruitful service provider. Gather the stories of personal journeys and professional journeys within your change initiative. Find ways to continue sharing these stories, within the agency and with other agencies, counties, and states. We are never learning on our own. Becoming more human is an effort that needs every soul and sector. If we gather, weave, and share our stories beautifully, mutual care becomes a sacred tribal warming blanket. A blanket of honor that we wrap around ourselves as we go.

SEEDS

Some kind of breeze moves through every soul, through every system. What matters is to take control of what this breeze carries. In nature, wind can carry pollution, allergens, toxins, and contagion. Or it can carry seeds. If your personal or system breeze can be filled with seeds, you're on the right path. With seeds, new beauty and wellness can take hold in the soil of mentality. Eventually, an entirely new forest or garden can grow. An outside source can introduce the seeds, or at least the germinating factors for your own seeds; but in the end, you must do the gardening, the reforesting. It must be done through internal work, not a strategy of accumulating external expertise. Too many systems fail this way in their effort to heal. Believe in the nature of seeds and their carriage system: the social breeze so pervasive in our impressionable lives.

A THIRD INTELLIGENCE

A great challenge sits at the center of this work, a seed of greatness. The challenge is to form a relationship in which servant and served create a third intelligence, a combined capacity for vision, dream, possibility, purpose. This third intelligence is fertile ground for the rising of an intimacy of brainstorming, a partnership of artistry, a co-authorship of promise. Within this third intelligence, the servant becomes as aware as possible of the reality, capacity, and giftedness of the served. The served becomes enlightened to the same in the servant. We can feel the aura of a third intelligence when it exists in an organization. It is the spirit of true communion, an open, flowing energy that feels like creativity because it is. The energy of an agency dictating to children, adults, and families is a heavy, constipated energy. Nothing is truly flowing, especially from the giftedness of those being served. This is the nature of oppression. Oppression imagines itself to be a savior, when in fact it is a destroyer. Of self-determination and freedom.

The energy of a third intelligence feels free and light and flowing because this is the nature of inspiration. Something has been ignited in the one being served. That fire is invited to ignite something in the servant, who in turn ignites something in the tribe, in the agency. This third intelligence does not reside in the exclusive chambers of authority and executive management. It does not reside in any one person or position. It lives in the air of the tribe, inhaled and exhaled into renewal by each member. It is the very climate. This allows it to remain as people come and go from the work. A third intelligence does not act like information-based competency. It does not go away when leadership and workers go away. It does not freeze in fear when the information changes, as it always will. It is not dependent upon present conditions in the community or culture. Third intelligence is an atmosphere of continuously regenerating inspiration, drawn from the well water of every person in the circle, regardless of servant or served status. People dream of working within an atmosphere of third intelligence. They dream of being cared for and supported in their times of need by a third intelligence. Everyone is waiting for this gathering of goodness and inspiration. Few realize that they themselves are the source they seek.

EVIDENCE OF YOUR TOUCH

Your moment together with someone you serve may be brief. Their struggle may be acute or chronic, but it is their journey. Yours can take you quickly from their life space on to your next person or circumstance. This leaves you without evidence of that person's outcome. Immediate gratification is not necessarily a part of your work. Not in the sense of seeing the ultimate destination of healing and wholeness. However, immediate gratification is available. If you are connected to your true purpose, you are fulfilled simply knowing that you have served. That you have given what you have, done what you can. You have poured compassion and caring, through your skillset and innovation. Evidence of your touching of another life can be found in how you feel about the way you touched. Your discernment and conscience know what you have done. Search your intuition and sensitivity. Have faith that your caring was a real thing, with real impact. Ours is not to control or shape lives, but to provide to those lives what they need to shape themselves. The evidence you seek is found in your own heart. In the way you sleep at night, wake in the morning, and move through your day.

Sometimes, you get to see the miracle that has happened. You run into someone whose life was saved or changed by you. Tears spill from their gratitude cup. They bear hug you. Or they write to you, letting you know of your legend in their life. You collect these thank-you notes because they mean something to you. Let your servitude mean just as much. Collect your memories and feelings in a way that feeds you. Your deepening awe and humility before the work, your aura of Grace, is all the evidence a purposeful you will need.

WHAT CAN BE

Our workplace does not have to be a dungeon, and we do not have to be its morose dungeon guards. We have it in us to change the culture. It is possible for the places where we work and serve to feel like an artist colony. A workshop where compassion sparks fly, a bright fireworks to our passionate industry. Those who work here and come here to be aided can feel the warmth of our caring, liberated by our own permission to let our truer rivers flow. Love and kindness only feel ridiculous to those who suffer in the grip of trauma's abject poverty of the soul. When we are flourishing, even in the midst of other people's crises, Love and kindness feel like home. We go there naturally.

In this uncompromised state, all our gifts emerge, the ones this servitude requires. We weave strands of caring relationship into the kind of touching that changes lives. What we feel in our heart for others causes us to be there for them in a healing way. What we feel in our heart for ourselves ignites us into a deeper care for our being. Two streams begin to feed each other: The sublime pain and joy of our work deepens us into a greater compassion, which we use as our vocational fire. A fire that burns away our shallowness. We emerge from the ashes of each difficult moment with tribal scars only this work can imbue. Scars that serve as memory: *This human thing we do is sacred.*

This cause is worthy of all that we give from the purity of our true nature. It is our nature that must be protected, not the hurtfulness we have mistaken for this work. We began as children, stricken with a pure pain when others pained, with robust joy when others exuded happiness. Now here we are, blessed and ordained to be the ones to whom suffering turns. What astounding Grace. What Hope murmurs in us is true: The goodness that is our most abiding nature can be resurrected from our childhood. We can heal and beautify our calling, both in act and spirit. And, further, in the bounty we bring to every heart and home.

Jaiya John is a doctor of social psychology, and has addressed over half a million professionals, adults, and youth worldwide. He was born and raised in New Mexico, and has lived in various locations, including Nepal. He is the author of numerous books, and is the founder of Soul Water Rising, a global human mission that supports the healing and wholeness of vulnerable populations.

Jacqueline V. Richmond and Kent W. Mortensen graciously, faithfully, and skillfully served as editors for *Your Caring Heart*.

Jaiya John titles are available where books are sold. Book revenue supports our global youth development programming, including our scholarship and book donation programs for displaced and vulnerable youth.

SECURE A JAIYA JOHN KEYNOTE, TALK, OR SEMINAR:

speaking@soulwater.org

To subscribe to our literary journal, *SOUL BLOSSOM*, please visit soulwater.org. *Soul Blossom* offers ongoing news of our global human mission, new book release notices, speaking engagement insights, and invited literary contributions. *Soul Blossom* is also a gathering space for the writing and artwork of young people from around the world.

OTHER BOOKS BY JAIYA JOHN

To learn more about this and other books by Jaiya John, to order discounted bulk quantities, or to learn about Soul Water Rising's global work, please visit us at:

soulwater.org

jaiyajohn.com

facebook.com/jaiyajohn

youtube.com/jaiyajohn

@jaiyajohn (instagram & twitter)

CPSIA information can be obtained
at www.ICGtesting.com
Printed in the USA
FSOW01n1231040816
23391FS